Dedicated with love and gratitude to my parents, Enda and Vera O'Boyle.

Chess

© Copyright Úna O Boyle

All rights reserved. No part of this book may be used or reproduced in any manner whatsoever without prior written permission from the author.

ISBN 13: 978-0-9929672-0-8

Author: Úna O Boyle

Graphics: Úna O Boyle

Illustrator: Noel Long

Publisher: GingerGM; www.gingergm.com; sales@gingergm.com

Unit 9, Trident Industrial Estate, Blackthorne Road, Colnbrook, Berkshire, SL3 0AX

Printer: Brunswick Press Ireland

Date: 2014

© Úna O Boyle

www.unaoboyle.net

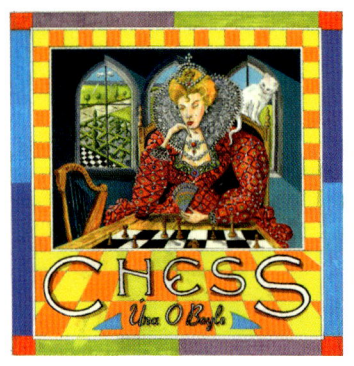

CHESS - 2014

FICHEALL - 2010

Illustrator: Noel Long

www.noellong.com

Introduction

Without a doubt chess is the most brilliant and beautiful board game ever invented! Hundreds and thousands of books are available in many different languages on different aspects of the game. This book is an adapted translation of the first ever chess book written in the Irish language called "Ficheall" - the Irish word for chess. Translated by the original author Úna O Boyle, "Ficheall" was shortlisted for Children's Book of the Year, Gradam Réics Carló in 2011.

This book will give you the tools to play chess and explore tactics and strategies in five sections:

Section 1: Page 1
Chess - The Game, The Pieces, Value of the Pieces, Aim of the Game.
In this section you will learn the basic rules of chess, how the pieces move, the "power" of the pieces and the aim or objective of the game. There are examples of simple games and positions which will help you understand chess and how to get to grips with basic chess tactics.

Section 2: Page 35
Notation, Check & Checkmate, Special Moves, Chess Etiquette, Games Ending in a Draw.
In these chapters you will learn about special rules and how to write down the moves. Most importantly you will also learn about the magic "Checkmate". If you wish to participate in a chess competition, it is important to know all the information in this section.

Section 3: Page 73
The Opening, Tactics & Strategy, The Passed Pawn, The Greek Gift, The Endgame,
Chess Players on Different Levels, A Game from Bobby Fischer.
You will get more ideas on the intricacies of chess here and it will take you some time to absorb all of the information in this section. But it's well worth it; you never know, it may launch you on a journey to becoming a chess master. Read and read again. When you have mastered this section you'll be amazed at the improvement in your chess playing skills. At this stage be careful as it's very probable that you will be bitten by the chess bug! The power of this bug will drive you to improve your skills through studying the famous games of the great chess masters. You can find lots of games from chess masters in books or on the internet. As bugs go, it's a very pleasant bug!

Section 4: Page 111
A Real Game, More Puzzles, Puzzles & Lessons - Answers,
Chess Puzzle from New Zealand.
It is now time for serious study. A great way to improve your game is to study classical games from the grandmasters around the world. I'm hoping that this book will inspire people of all ages to learn the beautiful game of chess and perhaps begin the journey of becoming grandmasters of the future.

Section 5: Page 145
Chess Terms, Chess in Different Languages, Reference Material.
Here you will find an explanation of important terms in chess. You will also find an interesting dictionary of chess in different languages.

This book is written for enthusiasts of all ages: for the young idealist who has no knowledge of chess, for the sharp competitor who wishes to improve his / her skills, for the ambitious player who wishes to participate in tournaments nationally and abroad - and of course, to win! The information in these pages will give you a flying start towards mastering chess. Improvement will happen gradually so be patient. There are lots of puzzles and games for you to explore on your learning journey. Enjoy!

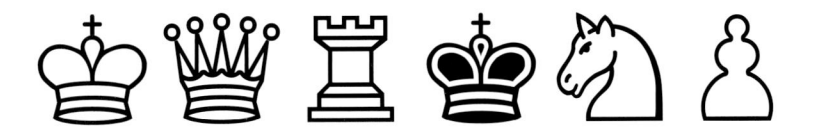

Foreword

It is a great pleasure for me to write the foreword to the English language edition of Úna O Boyle's lovely book. I have always felt affection for Ireland, perhaps in part because my maternal great-grandmother, Bedelia Kennedy, who died at the tragically young age of 24, hailed from County Wicklow. My first ever trip abroad, at the age of 10, in the April of 1976, was to the Emerald Isle when I attended the 2nd Easter International Chess Congress in Dundrum. The following year I was back again, heading the English team at the Glorney Cup, in Gormanston, Meath. Subsequent visits across the Irish Sea were less frequent and confined to the odd simultaneous exhibition in, say, Belfast or Dublin, but in more recent times, I have become a happy, regular competitor at the Bunratty Festival.

Given that Ireland has produced some outstanding talents – Alexander McDonnell, who played a series of six epic matches against Louis Charles de la Bourdonnais, in 1834, and James Mason of Kilkenny, who became one of the world's leading players half a century later – it is perhaps surprising that it took until 2010 for someone to write a chess book in Gaelic. Úna O Boyle – a most vivacious and energetic member of her international team - has thus performed a very valuable service.

These days chess in schools is all the rage. It has proven, in hundreds of academic studies, in dozens of countries, over the last four decades that chess makes kids (and adults) smarter – improving concentration, logic, calculation and strategic planning. It most recently became part of the curriculum in Armenia, part of a growing trend, as the educational benefits are increasingly widely recognised. In the field of mental health, chess has been demonstrated to be remarkably effective in delaying the onset of Alzheimer's. While all this research is exciting, it overlooks the most important attribute of the game: chess is tremendous fun! That is why I began as a five year old and why I still love it now. If you get but a fraction of the pleasure I have derived from it in my life, you will be very well satisfied indeed.

Grandmaster Nigel Short MBE

Contents

Section 1
1. CHESS - THE GAME; BASIC TERMS — 3
2. THE PIECES — 7
3. THE VALUE OF THE PIECES — 29
4. THE AIM OF THE GAME — 33

Section 2
5. NOTATION — 37
6. CHECK & CHECKMATE — 39
7. SPECIAL MOVES — 57
8. CHESS ETIQUETTE — 65
9. GAMES ENDING IN A DRAW — 67

Section 3
10. THE OPENING — 75
11. TACTICS & STRATEGY — 81
12. THE PASSED PAWN — 93
13. THE GREEK GIFT — 99
14. THE ENDGAME — 103
15. CHESS PLAYERS ON DIFFERENT LEVELS — 105
16. A GAME FROM BOBBY FISCHER — 107

Section 4
17. A REAL GAME — 113
18. MORE PUZZLES — 127
19. PUZZLES & LESSONS - ANSWERS — 135
20. CHESS PUZZLE FROM NEW ZEALAND — 141

Section 5
21. CHESS TERMS — 147
22. CHESS IN DIFFERENT LANGUAGES — 151
23. REFERENCE MATERIAL — 153

Lessons and Puzzles

1. **LESSON 1: CHECK** — 18
2. **LESSON 2: MOVING THE PIECES 1** — 21
3. **LESSON 3: PAWN GAME** — 22
4. **LESSON 4: A GAME WITHOUT PAWNS** — 23
5. **LESSON 5: A PAWN GAME** (with Kings & with Rooks and Kings) — 24
6. **LESSON 6: MOVING THE PIECES 2** — 25
7. **LESSON 7: MOVING THE PIECES 3** — 26
8. **LESSON 8: THE VALUE OF THE PIECES** — 31
9. **LESSON 9: CHECKMATE PUZZLES** — 47
10. **LESSON 10: THE PAWN** — 87
11. **LESSON 11: TACTICS** — 89
12. **LESSON 12: PROMOTING THE PASSED PAWN: queening** — 97
13. **LESSON 13: THE PASSED PAWN in the End Game** — 97
14. **CHAPTER 18: MORE PUZZLES** — 127

Section 1

Chess - The Game - basic terms   3
The Pieces   7
Value of the Pieces   29
Aim of the Game   33

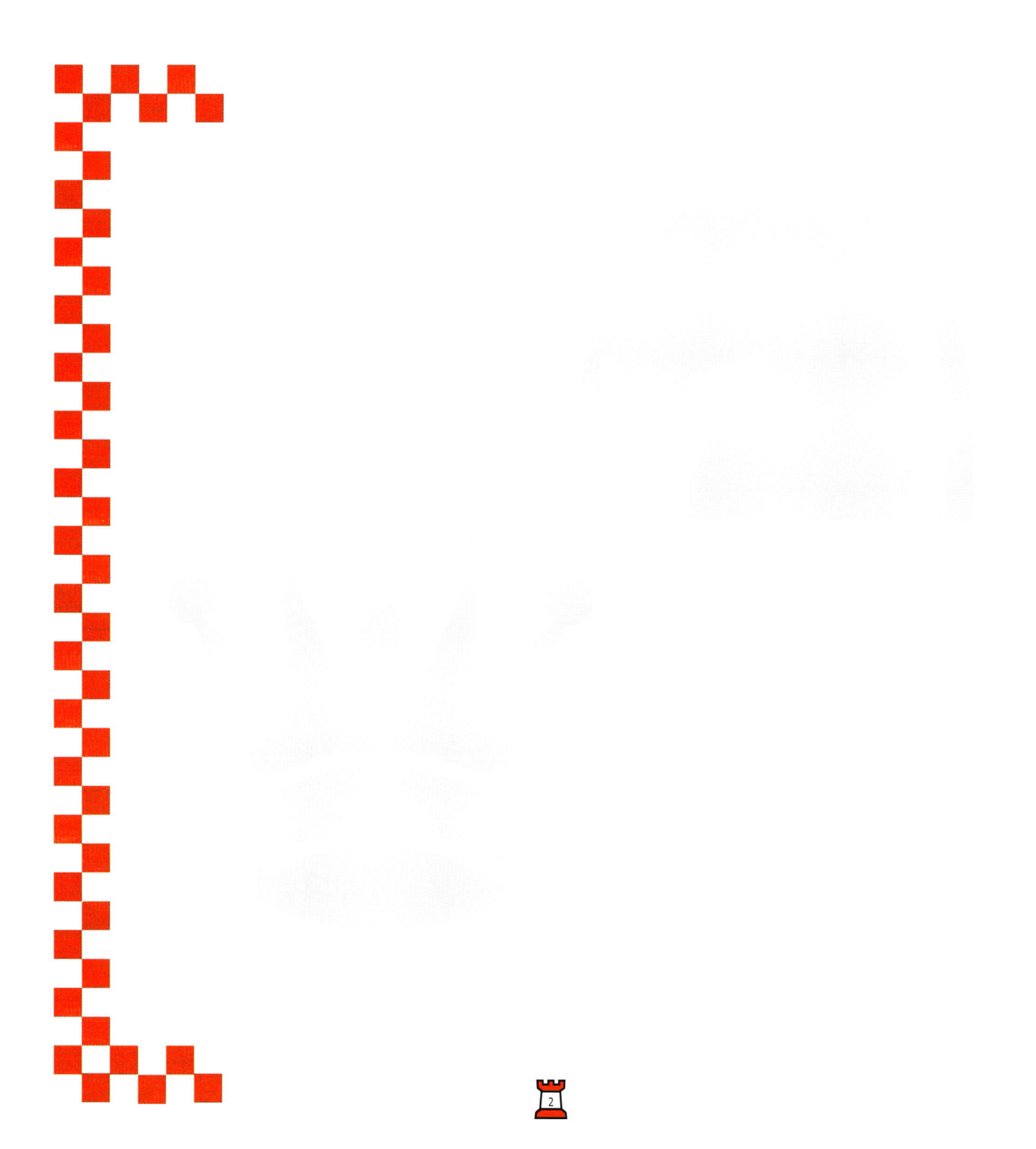

1
CHESS – THE GAME
BASIC TERMS

So you want to find out where the game of chess came from! Perhaps this is also a good time to learn some chess terminology.

The Game

Down through the millennia (thousands of years, tens of centuries) people have been playing chess. Chess originated in India and through the years found its way to every corner of the world. Over the years many rules of the original game have changed to create the game that exists today. Some say that chess is the most played game on the planet. There are even stories about the legendary Irish warrior, Cuchullann, playing chess! Well, that's why I love chess. It's a crazy and wonderful game: Two teams battling each other and skirmishes everywhere - the whole fight just to protect the king! Thanks be to goodness we don't have to do these things in real life to protect our presidents or prime ministers!

PAWN
QUEEN **KING** **BISHOP** **KNIGHT** **ROOK**

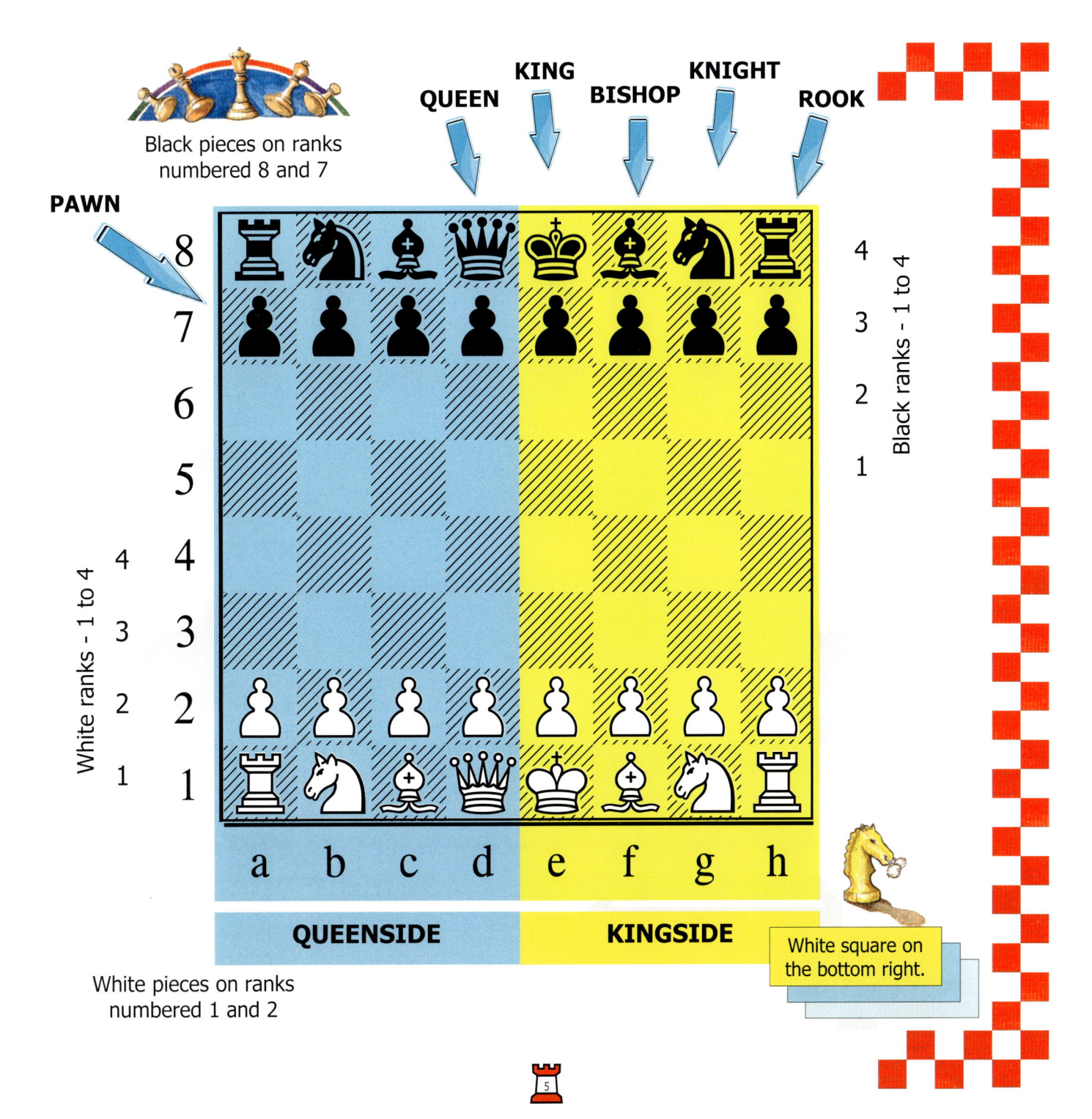

Black pieces on ranks numbered 8 and 7

White ranks - 1 to 4

Black ranks - 1 to 4

a b c d e f g h

QUEENSIDE **KINGSIDE**

White square on the bottom right.

White pieces on ranks numbered 1 and 2

Basic Terms

Firstly, here are a few important chess terms:

File, Rank, Diagonal

FILE

The squares running up and down the chess board.

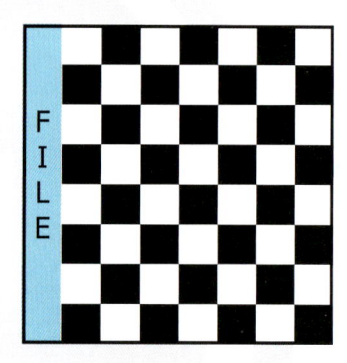

RANK

The squares running across the chess board.

DIAGONAL

The squares running diagonally across the chess board.

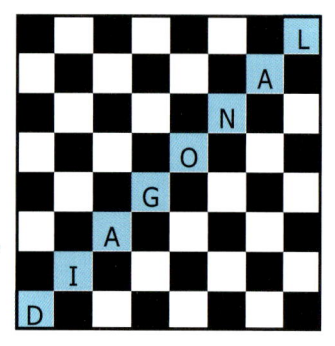

2
THE PIECES

It's now time to learn about the pieces.

THE PIECES

Chess is one of the oldest board games in the world. There are 32 pieces and a chess board in a chess set. The pieces represent the armies and the board represents the battlefield; there are no trees, rivers, valleys or buildings behind which to hide. This means you can control the events of the battle far better then any army general. It is how you manoeuvre your pieces that determines eventual victory - or defeat. There are two armies, one white and one black. The armies move towards each other and then the fight begins. Attacking and defending strategies are played out as though the players are real generals overseeing a real battle. The general with the best strategy and tactics should win the game.

The opposing armies are made up of the same number of pieces and pawns so the game begins on an equal footing:

**Eight Pawns, Two Knights, Two Bishops,
Two Rooks, King and Queen.**

The game begins on equal terms but a win or a loss depends on how the players move their pieces around the battlefield.

**Often chess players will use the word "piece"
for every chess piece except the pawn.**

Principal rules in laying down your chessboard:
The square on the **bottom right corner** must be **White - WHITE ON THE RIGHT.**

Also take note how the **white pieces begin on ranks 1 & 2** and the **black pieces begin on ranks 7 & 8.**

How the Pieces Move

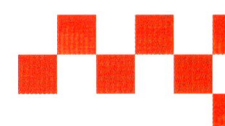

There are 16 pieces on each chess team.

In your army you have:
1 King, 1 Queen, 2 Bishops, 2 Knights, 2 Rooks and 8 Pawns

There are 16 black and 16 white pieces in a chess set.
Here are their names and symbols:

THE PIECES

♔ ♚ **KING**	One King
♕ ♛ **QUEEN**	One Queen
♗ ♝ **BISHOP**	Two Bishops
♘ ♞ **KNIGHT**	Two Knights
♖ ♜ **ROOK**	Two Rooks
♙ ♟ **PAWN**	Eight Pawns

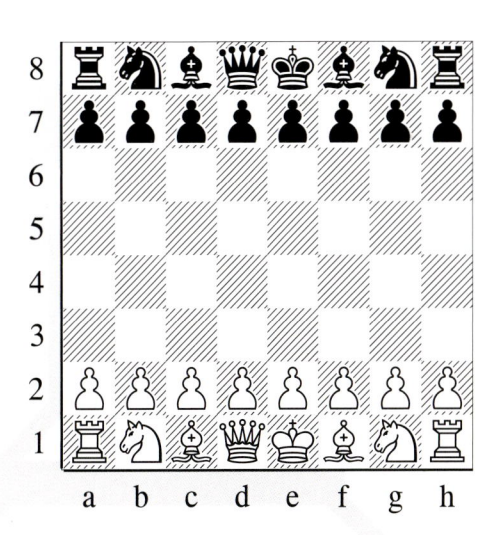

the PAWN

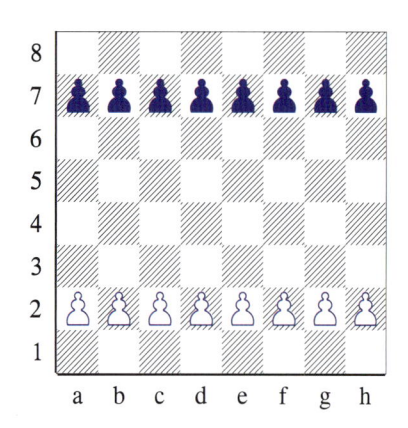

Each side has EIGHT **PAWNS**.
Here is where they are positioned at the beginning of the game.

When moving for the first time, each **PAWN** can move one square ahead **or** two squares ahead, you have a choice. But after the first move, the **PAWN** can only move one square ahead on any move.
PAWNS cannot jump over other pieces.

How the PAWN moves: On the first move each PAWN may move **one or two** squares ahead. After the first move it may only move **one** square ahead.

How The PAWN captures:
The PAWN captures in a different way to the way it moves.
The PAWN must move **one square diagonally forward** in order to capture.

THE CAPTURE:
An enemy piece is captured when you move your piece into a square occupied by the enemy piece. The King is the only piece that cannot be captured.

In diagram 1 on the right you can see how the White PAWN moves, and how it can capture an enemy piece:

- Bishop capture (diagonally to the left).
- Knight capture (diagonally to the right).

The PAWN has another option:
- It can move forward one square.

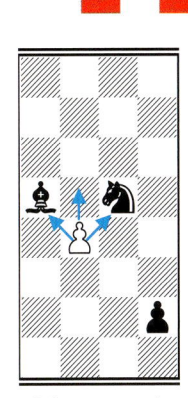

Diagram 1

At the same time WHITE must be careful as the BLACK **PAWN** is at the bottom of the board. BLACK is hoping to push the pawn to the final square where it can be converted to another piece. This a special pawn rule in chess which you will learn more about on page 60 "Pawn Promotion". Usually players change a **pawn** to a **queen** as it is the most powerful piece but you can also change it to a **knight**, **bishop** or **rook**.

In diagram 2 the white **PAWN** can capture the rook or the knight but it cannot move one square ahead in the direction of the bishop because the square is occupied.

PAWNS can only capture diagonally.

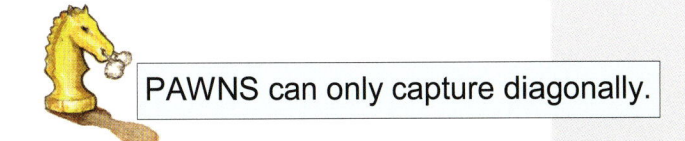

Diagram 2

In diagram 3 none of the **PAWNS** can move except the WHITE pawn on the top which can capture the BLACK rook.

Diagram 3

the KNIGHT

This is where the **KNIGHTS** are positioned at the beginning of the game.

The **KNIGHT** is the only piece that can jump over other pieces. In the diagram on the right the **KNIGHT** can jump over the pawns.

This is how the **KNIGHT** moves:

The **KNIGHT** moves in an "L" shape. It moves two squares in one direction and one square in another direction.

On the diagram on the right you can see how the **KNIGHT** may move into any square that has a **CROSS**.

A **KNIGHT** in the centre of the board is a very powerful piece reaching out like an octopus in eight different directions.

> The knight works best in the centre of the chess board. A knight on the side of the board has much less power.
> It is the only piece that can jump over other pieces.

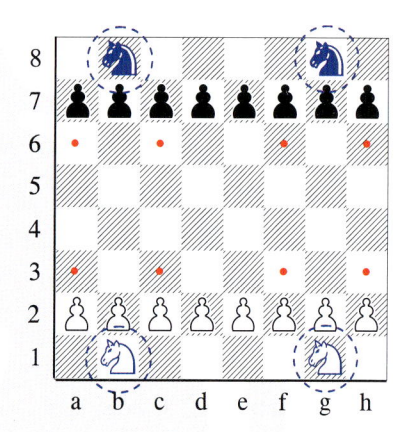

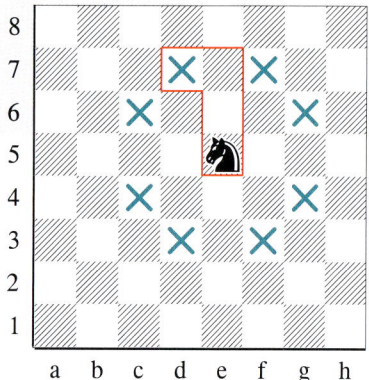

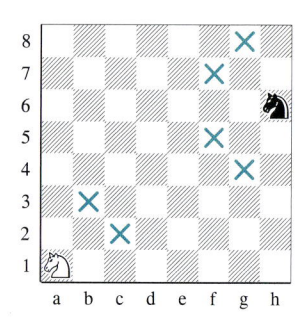

"A knight on the rim is very dim"

the BISHOP

This is where the **BISHOPS** are positioned at the beginning of a game.
They cannot jump over other pieces.

The **BISHOP** moves **diagonally**.

On the diagram on the right you can see how the **BISHOP** may move into any square that has a **CROSS**.

A **BISHOP** on an unblocked diagonal, anywhere on the board, is a very powerful piece.

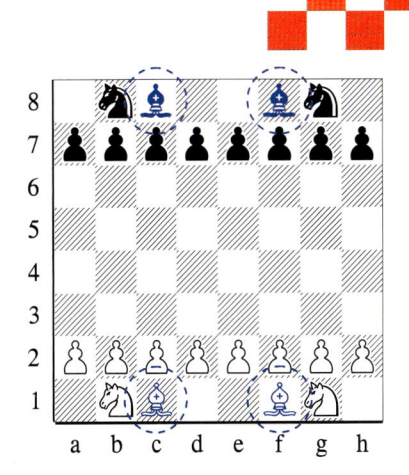

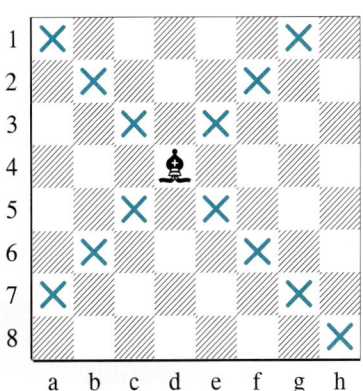

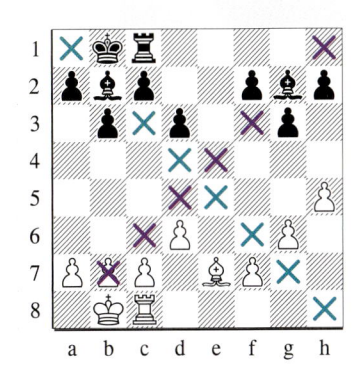

The bishop works well on a diagonal that is not blocked by black or white pawns.

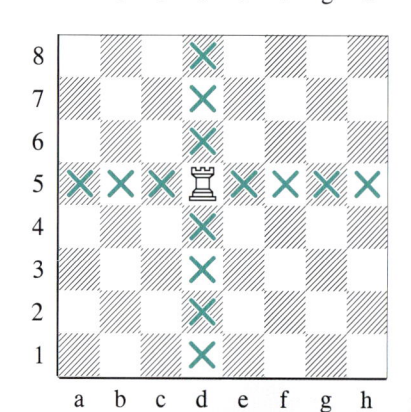

the ROOK

ROOKS are positioned at the four corners of the chess board at the beginning of the game.
The **ROOK** cannot jump over other pieces.

An old term for a ROOK is a CASTLE but in modern chess we usually call the piece a "ROOK".

This is how the **ROOK** moves:
The **ROOK** can move up, down or across the chess board, always in a straight line.

On the diagram on the left the **ROOK** can move into any square that has a **CROSS**.

A **ROOK** on an unblocked file is a very powerful piece. Two rooks working together on an unblocked file are like tanks in a convoy ready to demolish anything in their path. An unblocked file has no pieces or pawns occupying it.

If you place a rook on an unblocked file it has lots of powerful space. See "Open file" on page 84 for information on this important tactic.

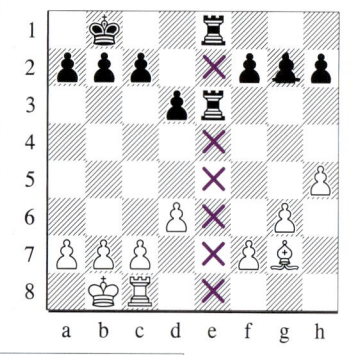

Rooks that work TOGETHER on a file or rank are very powerful.

the QUEEN

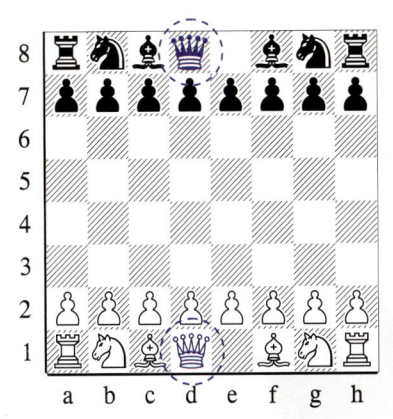

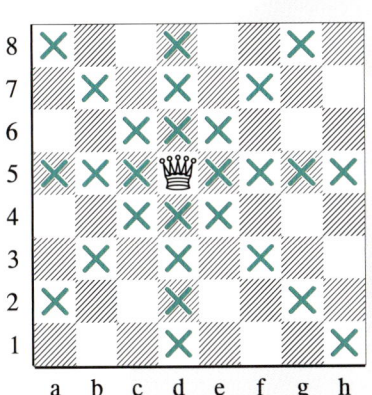

Here is where the **QUEENS** are positioned at the beginning of the game.
The **QUEEN** cannot jump over other pieces.

Take note that each **QUEEN** is positioned on the same coloured square as herself.

> i.e. **the black QUEEN** starts on a **black** square,
> the **White QUEEN** starts on a **white** square.

This is how the **QUEEN** moves:
The **QUEEN** can move up, down, across or diagonally on the chess board.

As you can see, she is the most powerful piece.

On the diagram on the left, the **QUEEN** can move into any square that has a **CROSS**.

At the beginning of a game
the black QUEEN starts on a black square.
the white QUEEN starts on a white square.

When beginning a game of chess
the **QUEEN** likes to be colour co-ordinated and so likes a throne the same colour as her dress!

The queen works very well with rooks on a file or rank or with a bishop on a diagonal.

the KING

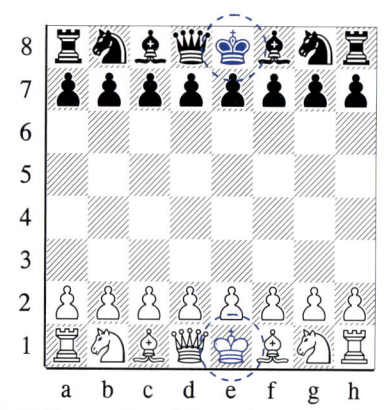

KINGS are positioned beside their queens at the beginning of the game.

The **KING** cannot jump over other pieces.

The diagram on the right shows how the **KING** moves:
One square in any direction.
The **KING** can move into any square that has a **CROSS**.

When the king is attacked by an enemy piece, this is called check. The **KING** cannot move into **check**.
This means that the **KING** cannot move into a square that the enemy is attacking.

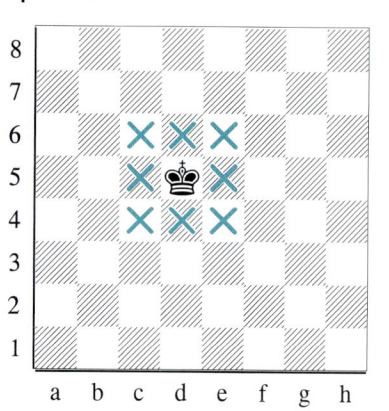

You cannot move into check. If you have made this move by mistake, you must return the move and make another move instead.

- **A KING cannot be positioned on a square directly beside the opposing KING.**
- **There must be at least one square between the WHITE and BLACK KING**
- **You cannot capture the KING at any time during the game.**
- **A KING can never move to a square that is being attacked or controlled by an enemy piece.**
- **The KING - The game:** The king is not the most powerful piece but it is without doubt the most important piece. The aim of the game is to place the enemy king in a CHECK that he cannot escape from, this is called checkmate. If an enemy piece is attacking a king, this is called "check". See Chapter 6, page 39, "Check & Checkmate", for full details on rules. The following page will give you some basic knowledge. On your journey in searching for a CHECKMATE you will be capturing your opponent's pieces and employing different strategies and tactics to give you stronger powers to do this.
- **The Aim of the game:** To trap the enemy king and deliver the final attack of "checkmate", an attack on your opponent's KING from which he cannot escape.

Check & Checkmate

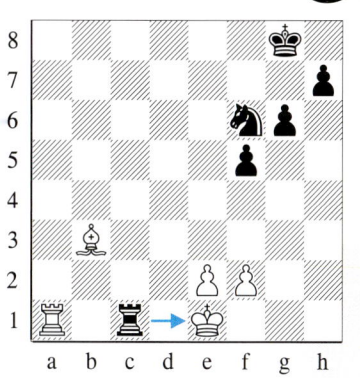

In the diagram on the left the **black rook** is attacking the **white king**. There is a special term for an attack on the king, it is called **"CHECK"**. It's not absolutely necessary to say it, but if both players are just starting out, it's no harm to say "check" to your opponent.

If the king is in **check** it must be moved from the attacking position **immediately**.

In the example on the left the black rook on c1 is checking the white king on e1. Note how each square is named by a letter corresponding to the letters on the bottom and a number corresponding to the numbers on the side.

If the king cannot escape from **CHECK**, this is **CHECKMATE** and the game is over, the winner is the player who has delivered **CHECKMATE**.

If you are in check you **must** save your king **immediately** and move out of check.

There are three ways to safely get a king out of **check**:

3 WAYS TO ESCAPE FROM CHECK
1. Move the king to a safe square (*Move*).
2. Capture the attacker (*Capture*).
3. Move a piece to a square between the enemy attacker and the king (*Block*).

Move - Capture - Block

How can the white king move out of check in the example above?
Before looking at the answers below see if you can find the answers yourself.
Use the name of the piece and the square in which it travels to, using the letter and number formula.

Move:
Capture:
Block:

1. **Move:** The white king can move to the square d2.
2. **Capture:** The white rook on a1 can capture the black rook on c1.
3. **Block:** The white bishop on b3 can move to d1 and block the check on the white king.

See Chapter 6, page 39, "Check & Checkmate", for a more comprehensive explanation.

Lesson 1 — Check

What white piece is placing the black king in check?

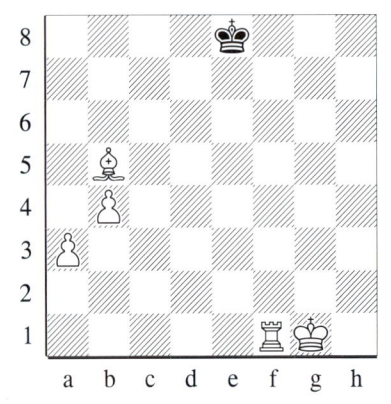

1

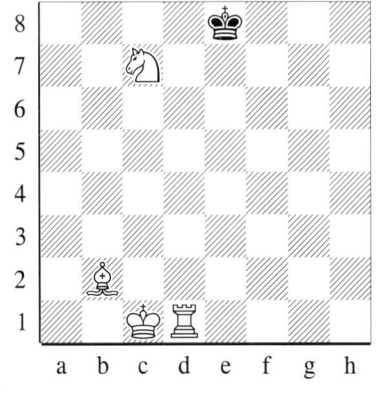

2

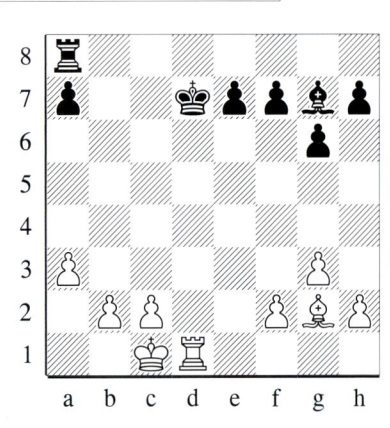

3

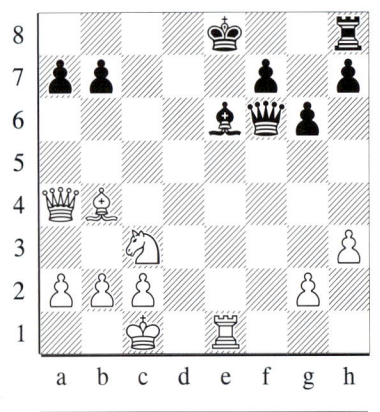

4

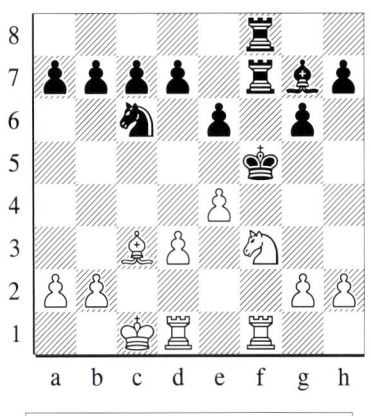

5

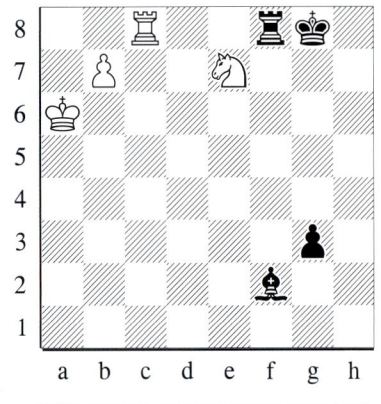

6

Castling

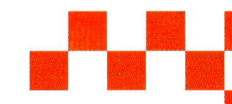

Castling is a special move in which two pieces, the king and the rook, move at the same time. You can only make this move once in any game.

This is the only time that the king is allowed to move two squares.
This is also the only time in which two pieces move at the same time.
When pieces between the **KING** and **ROOK** have been moved out, the king moves two squares in the direction of a rook and the rook then hops over him to the square right beside him: as simple as that!

See Chapter 7, page 57, "Special Moves", for a more comprehensive explanation.

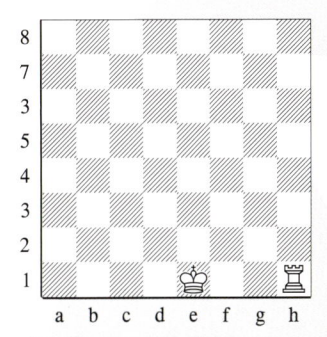

Before castling on the Kingside

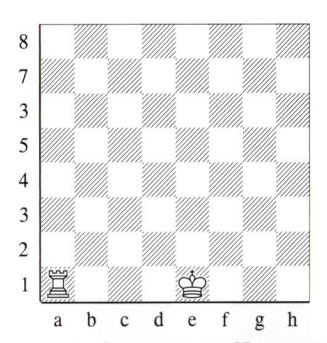

Before castling on the Queenside

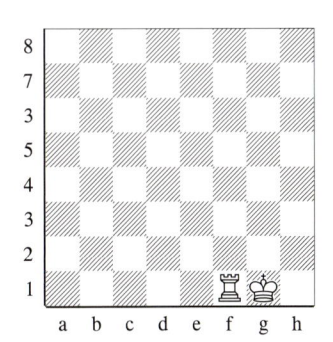

After castling on the Kingside

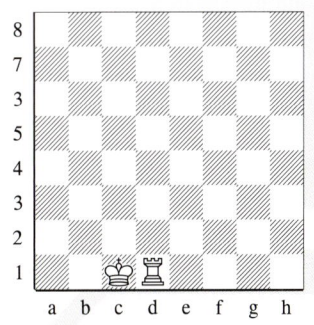

After castling on the Queenside

How to Capture Pieces

Naturally two pieces cannot occupy the same square. So what happens if there is already a piece on a square that you wish to occupy? If an enemy piece occupies the square that you want to move to, you may remove this enemy piece from the game and place your piece in that square. This is called capturing or killing. If the square is occupied by another of your own pieces then you cannot place your piece in that square. You are not allowed to capture your own pieces, that's your opponent's privilege!

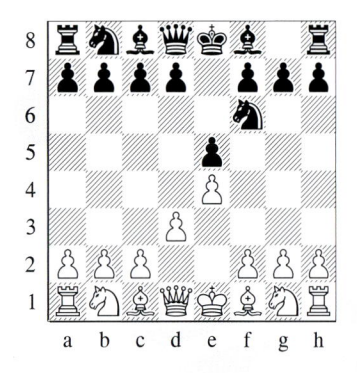

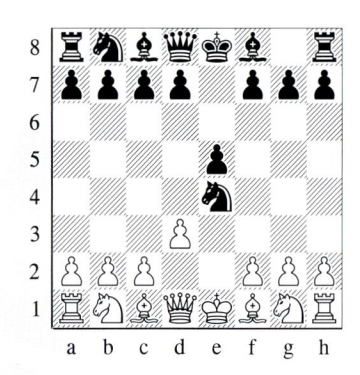

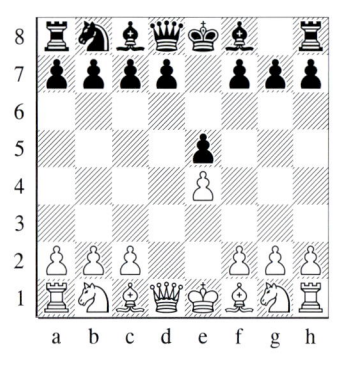

1: The black knight on f6 captures the pawn on e4.

2: The White pawn on d3 captures the knight on e4.

Capturing a piece: In order to capture a piece, you may place your own piece in the square that an opponent's piece occupies and remove that enemy piece.

Moving the Pieces 1 — Lesson 2

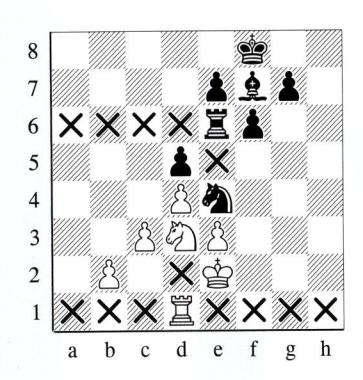

1. An X is placed in each square in which the black and white rook can be placed.

2. Place an X on each piece that the black bishop on e6 can capture.

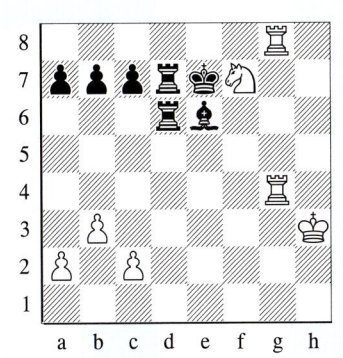

3. Place an X on any square that the white queen on b8 can move to without fear of capture by a black queen.

4. Place an X on any square that the knights are able to occupy. Use a different colour for each knight.

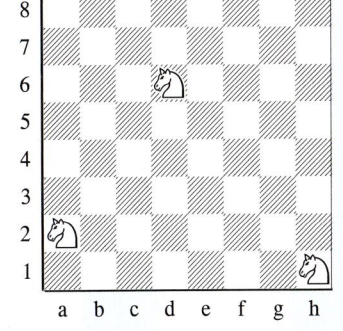

5. Place an X on any square that the white queen on d5 can enter safely without being attacked by an enemy piece.

6. Place an X on any square that the black rook on d6 can enter safely without being attacked by an enemy piece.

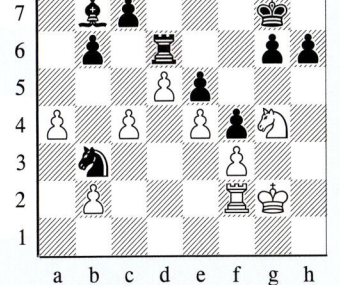

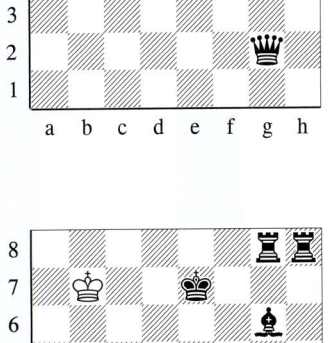

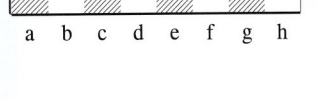

Lesson 3
A Pawn Game

Before playing this game check out the rule "Pawn Promotion" on page 60.

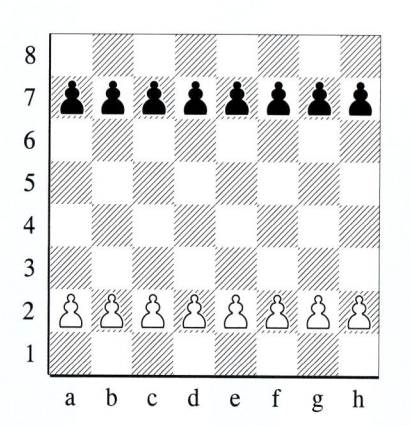

Play this game with a friend, using only the pawns. This will give you a firm idea of how pawns move, capture and promote. When a pawn reaches the end of the board and can go no further you may exchange it for another piece. This is called promotion or queening. As the queen is the most powerful piece it is most common that the pawn is replaced with a queen on promotion. The winner of this game is the first to cross the board and promote. The rule of "Pawn Promotion" is fully explained on page 60.

Don't be shy in being a little crafty while trying to promote your pawn!

EXAMPLE OF A PAWN GAME:

1. White begins, pushing the d-pawn forward two squares towards the centre.

2. Black mirrors white's first move. Both pawns are now firmly rooted on the d-file, neither pawn can move forward.

3. White moves another pawn forward two squares. Is this a mistake? Black can capture the e-pawn.

4. Black captures the white pawn on e4.

5. White moves a pawn up one square and lays down a challenge to the advancing black pawn. Will Black capture again on f3?

6. Good move! Black moves forward. Now the black pawn cannot be stopped and the pawn will be promoted.

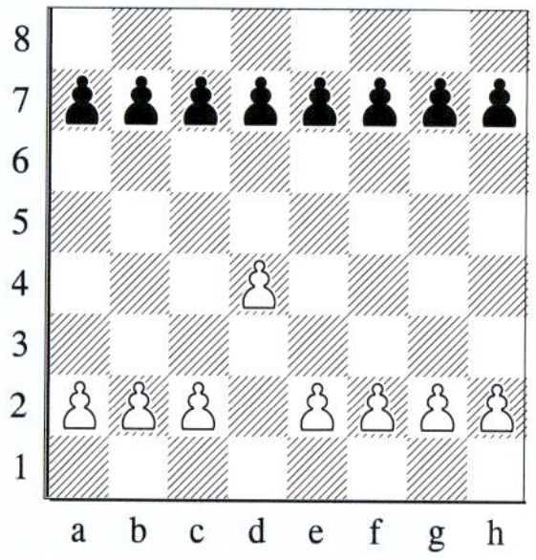

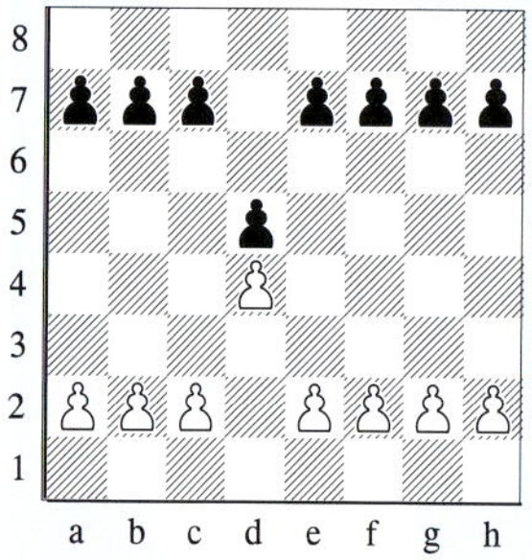

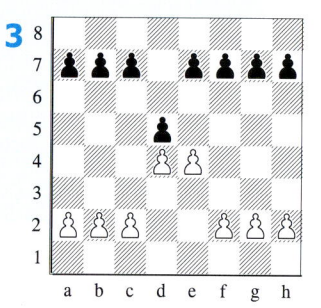

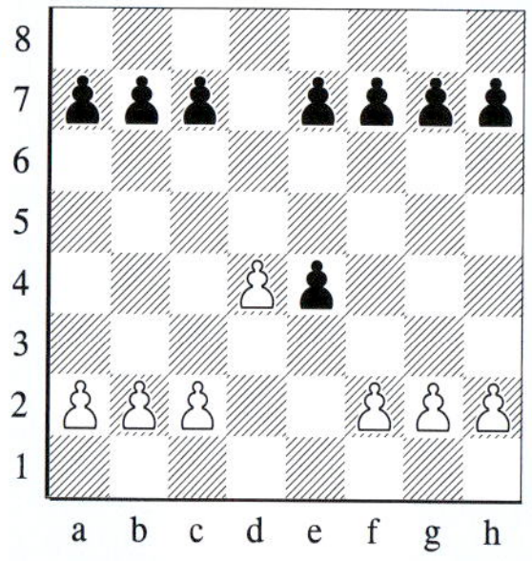

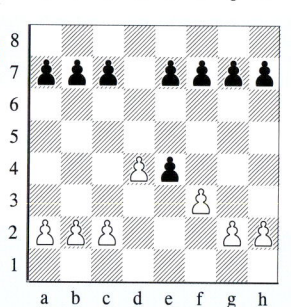

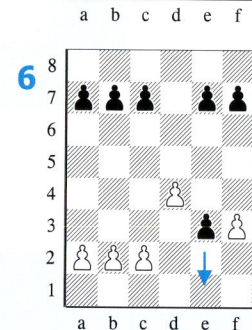

Lesson 4

A Game without Pawns

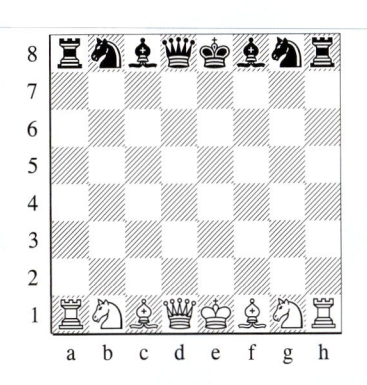

Play this game with a friend, with only the main pieces. This game will give you a good feel for how pieces move and also how pieces capture each other. The winner is the first player to capture all of his / her opponent's pieces - apart from the king, as you cannot ever capture the king!

1. **White** begins and quickly discovers that there is a free piece on offer: The white rook on a1 captures the black rook on a8.
2. **Black** gives White a dose of the same medicine on the kingside when Black captures the white rook to win a piece. The black rook on h8 captures the white rook on h1.

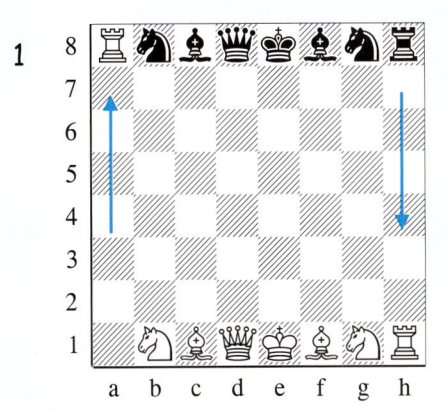

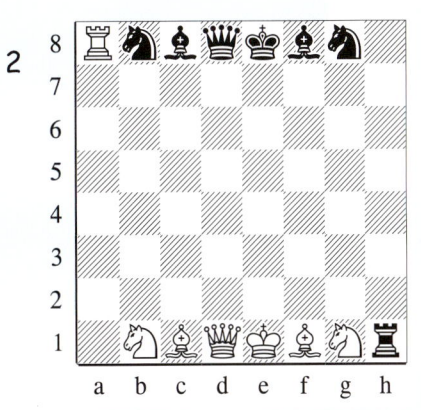

Make sure that pieces protect each other during the game. Watch that your opponent cannot easily capture pieces from your army. I don't think I should say any more at this stage. It's now time to play a game of chess without using any of the pawns.

-ENJOY!

Lesson 5

A Pawn Game

1. with Kings   **2.** with Rooks and Kings

Learn about the power of the rooks and the power of the king.

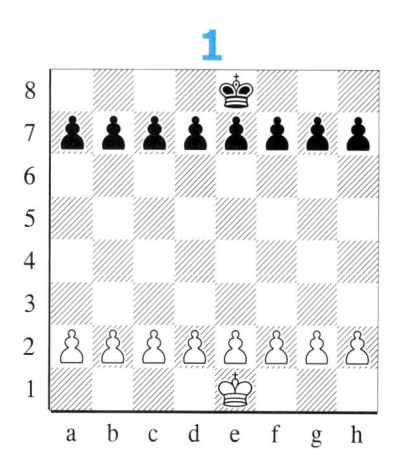

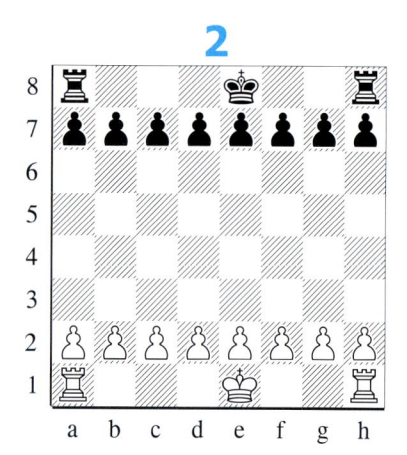

Play these games with a friend:

1. The first game playing with pawns and kings only;
2. The second game playing with the pawns, rooks and kings.

These games will give you a good idea of how pieces move, the way in which pieces capture and how you can get an extra queen with the help of a pawn.
Use the "en passant" rule this time which is explained fully on page 62.

The winner is the first player to promote the pawn to a queen that is not immediately captured after promotion or the player who delivers checkmate.

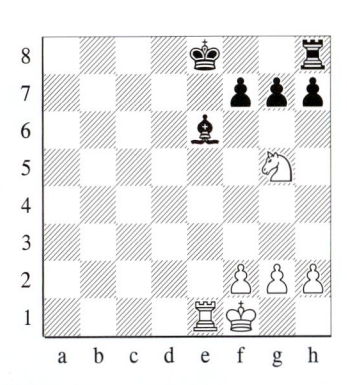

Moving the Pieces 2 — Lesson 6

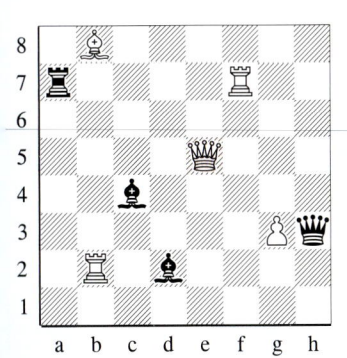

1 Put an X in any square into which the white queen on e5 can move safely without being attacked by an enemy piece.

2 Put an X in any square into which the black knight on f7 can jump to without being attacked by an enemy piece.

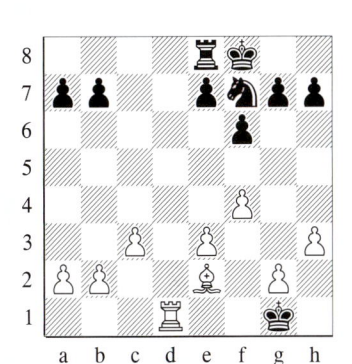

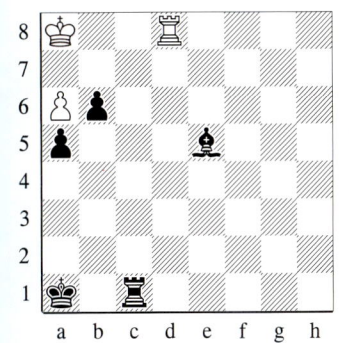

3 Put an X in any square into which the white king on a8 can go to without moving into check.

4 Put an X in any square into which the white king on a1 can enter legally. **Be careful!**

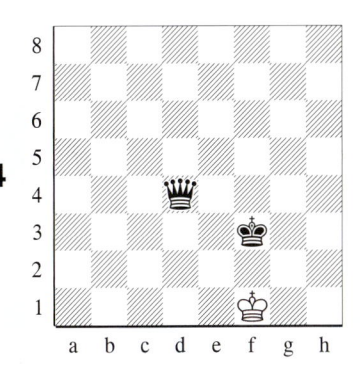

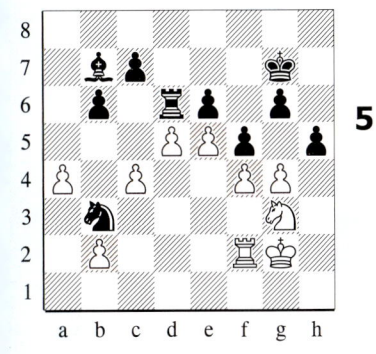

5 Put an X in any square where a white pawn can capture a piece or another pawn. **Be careful!**

6 Put an X in any square into which the black bishop can enter. **Again, be careful!**

25

Moving the Pieces 3

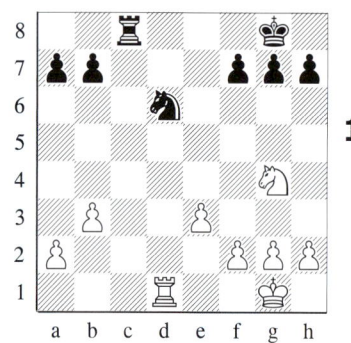

Lesson 7

1 Put an X on any white piece that can place the black king on g8 in **CHECK**.

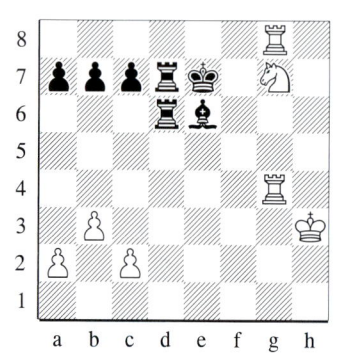

2 Put an X on any white piece that can place the black king on e7 in **CHECK**.

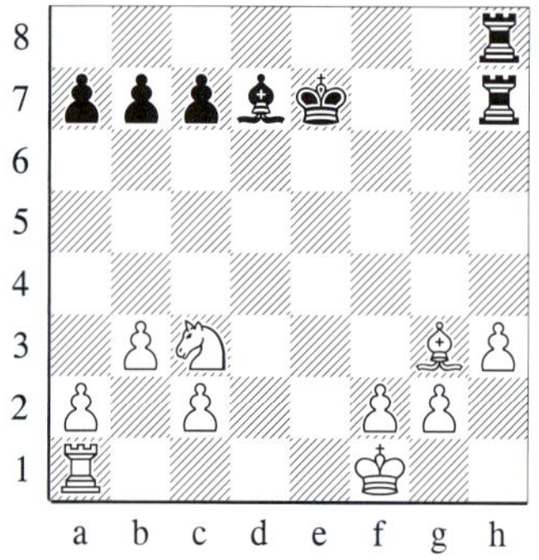

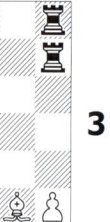

3 Put an X on any white piece that can place the black king on e7 in **CHECK**.

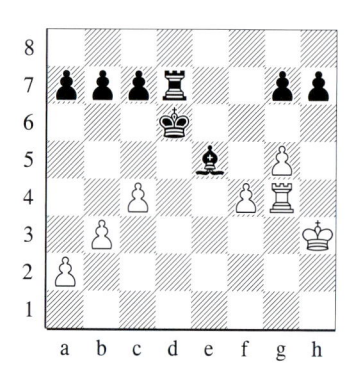

4 Put an X on any white piece or pawn that can place the black king on d6 in **CHECK**.

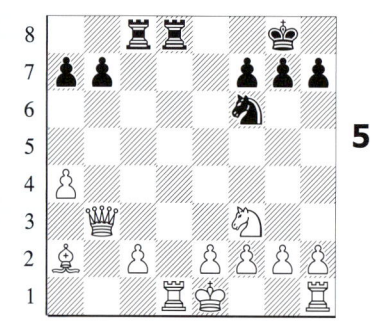

5 Put an X on any white piece that can place the black king on g8 in **CHECK**.

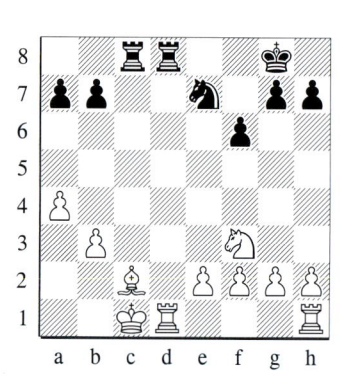

6 Put an X on any white piece that can place the black king on g8 in **CHECK**.

The Power of the Rook and The Power of the King

Here are a few pointers on the power of the ROOK and the power of the KING:

1. Rooks work very well together. Rooks also work well with the queen.
2. The rook works best on an unblocked file ("open file" and "half-open file", page 84).
3. Develop rooks: bring them out and use them.
4. Doubled rooks on an unblocked file are very powerful.
5. Always take note of the mobility of yours and your opponent's pieces.
6. A rook on the seventh rank, attacking your opponents pawns, is very powerful.
7. A rook behind a pawn moving up the board looking to promote (a passed pawn) gives it extra strength. ("The Passed pawn", page 93).
8. Block your opponent's passed pawn with your king. Stop it from promoting by putting your king in front of it.
9. Don't forget that your king is a piece, a piece with power.
10. The king is best in hiding for most of the game. At the end of a game, if the queens have been captured, the king must come out to work attacking your opponent's pieces and protecting your own. Kings are particularly useful in capturing pawns at the end of a game so set your king some tasks when the queens are off the board.

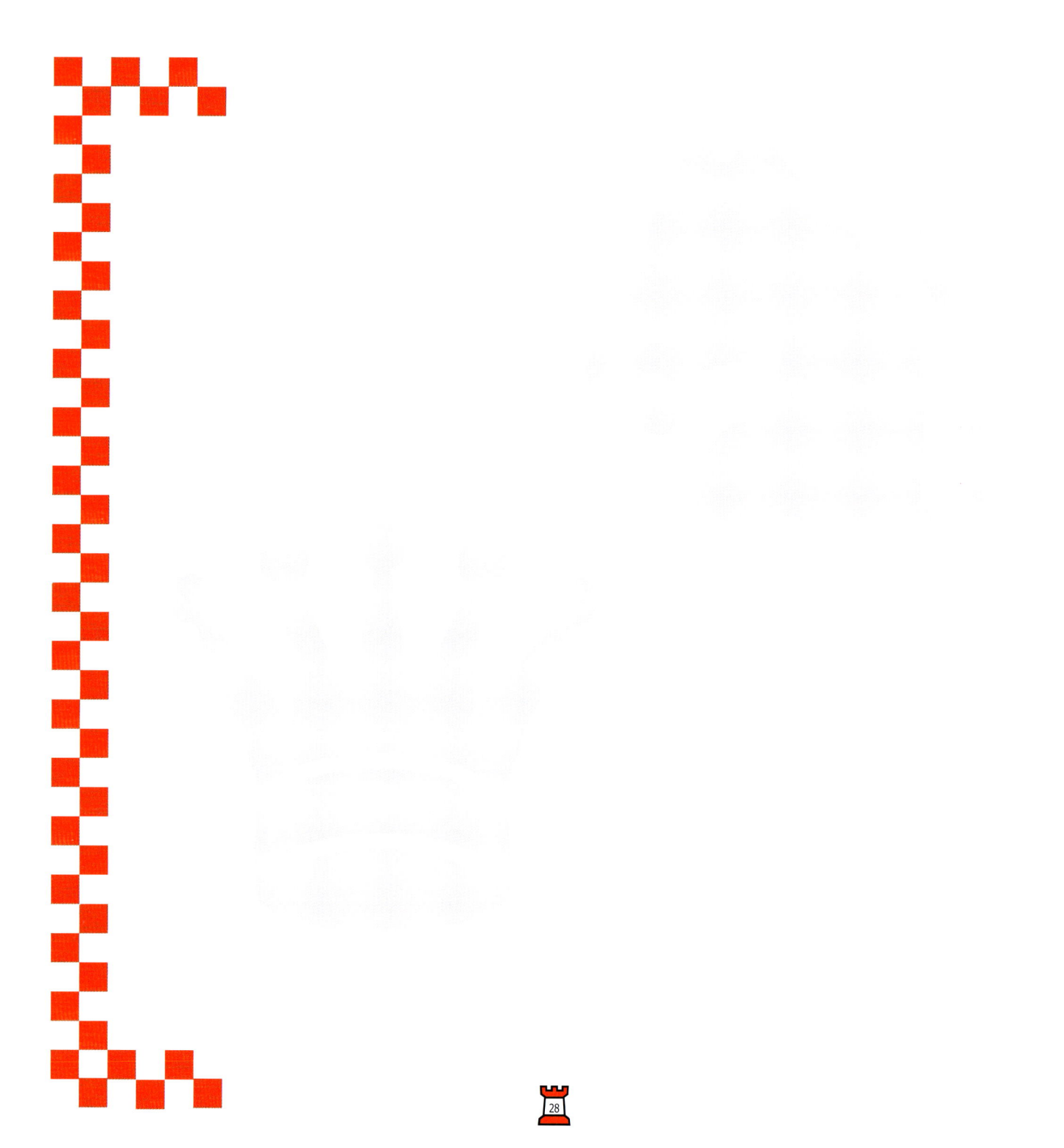

3
VALUE OF THE PIECES

By placing virtual points onto each piece we understand their power a little more.

Value of the Pieces

In chess there are no actual points awarded to pieces. This system of giving points to pieces is simply a way to help you understand their individual power. It will help you in determining whether an exchange of pieces is a good thing based on their numerical power.

KING — **No points** (= the game)

The most important piece.
The King remains in hiding most of the time.

QUEEN — **Nine** points

The Queen is the strongest and most powerful piece.
(Well, she is a woman after all!?)

BISHOP — **Three** points

The Bishop must get out of bed and be at work very early.

KNIGHT — **Three** points

The Knight must be ready to hop into battle at a moment's notice.

ROOK — **Five** points

Rooks work well together or with the Queen.

PAWN — **One** point

The smallest and least powerful piece.
The pawns take very good care of the king.
Pawns can also change into queens, rooks, bishops or knights, so look after them well!
("Pawn Promotion", page 60)

KING	the game
QUEEN	9
ROOK	5
BISHOP	3
KNIGHT	3
PAWN	1

Lesson 8
Value of the Pieces

What are the missing pieces below?

1. ♙ = ♙
2. ♗ = ♘
3. ♕ = ♖ + ♗ + ♙
4. ♖ = ♗ + ? + ?
5. ♗ = ? + ? + ?
6. ♝ + ♞ = ? + ?
7. ♛ + ♞ = ♜ + ? + ♙ + ♙
8. ♜ + ♞ = ♟ + ♟ + ? + ?
9. ♞ + ♝ = ♜ + ?
10. ♝ = ♙ + ♙ + ?
11. ♛ = ♙ + ♘ + ?
12. ♜ + ♝ + ♟ = ?
13. ♜ + ♟ = ? + ♘
14. ♜ + ♝ + ♞ = ♕ + ? + ?
15. ♛ + ♟ = ? + ?
16. ♟ + ? = ♗ + ?
17. ♜ + ♜ = ? + ?
18. ♞ + ♞ = ♗ + ? + ? + ?
19. ♟ + ♟ + ♞ + ♝ + ♞ + ♝ = ♖ + ?

1. ...... Pawn ......
2. ...... Knight ......
3. ...... Bishop + Pawn ......
4. ....
5. ....
6. ....
7. ....
8. ....
9. ....
10. ....
11. ....
12. ....
13. ....
14. ....
15. ....
16. ....
17. ....
18. ....
19. ....

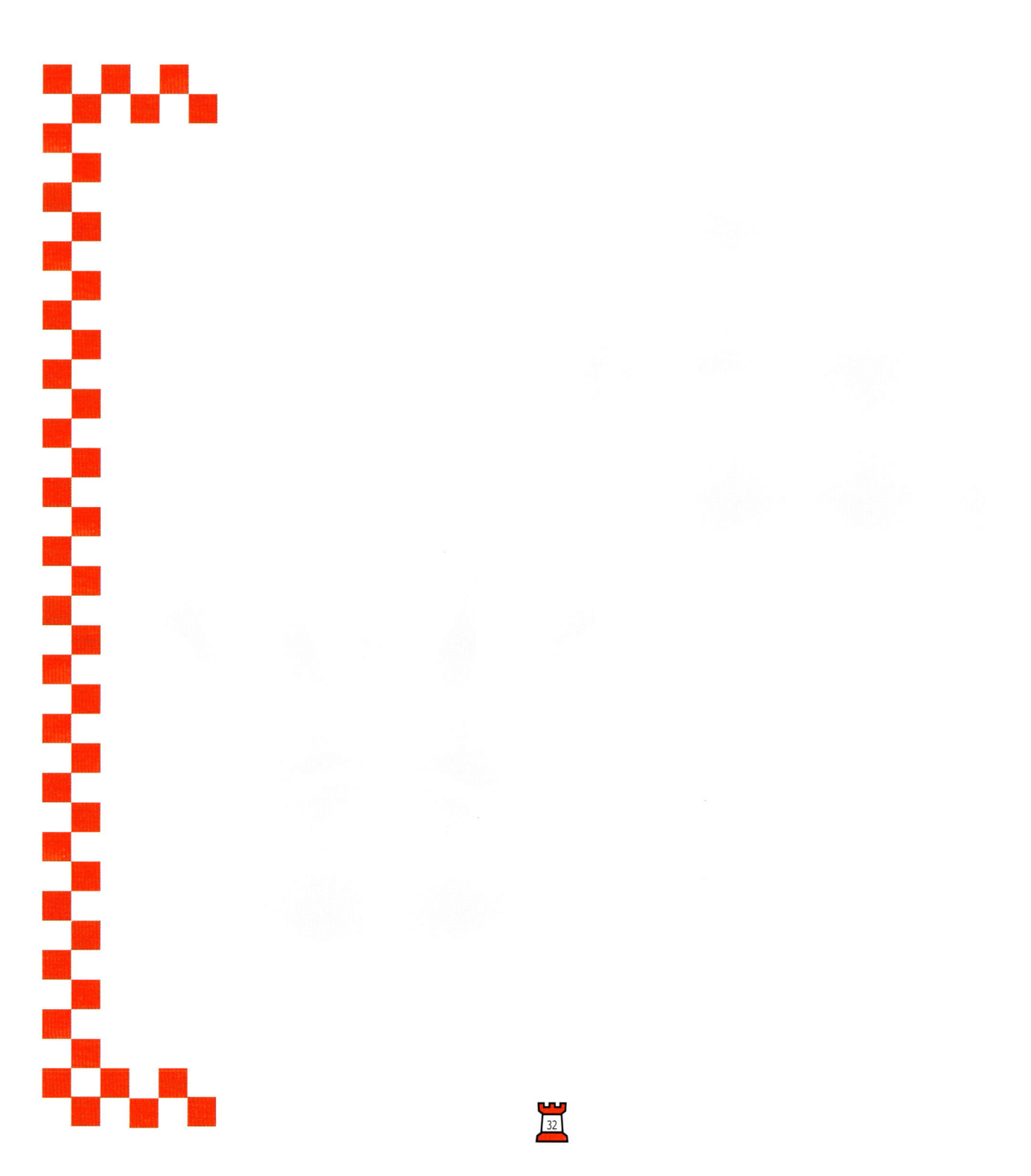

4
AIM OF THE GAME

So, what's the story about playing chess?
How do you win?

Aim of the Game

Put simply, the aim of chess is to trap your opponent's king and deliver checkmate. However, actually doing this is not so simple. Chess is a battle of wits between two players, each controlling his / her own army. The battle can last for hours or end very suddenly and quickly. You can gain the advantage by steady pressure, building up your attack slowly by capturing enemy pieces while keeping your own pieces safe. A well aimed blow after only a few moves can also end a game.

Though checkmate is the aim of the game, one of the ways you can achieve this is by weakening your enemy's army through capturing their pieces or restricting the movement of their pieces. The idea is that your opponent will then be too weak to resist attack, and will not be able to defend the king easily. Players must first compete for a good position in the **middle of the board**. One player will get the upper hand and will then be able to invade enemy territory, capture weak enemy pieces, or open up a decisive attack on the enemy king.

What's the Aim of the Game?
Simply trap your opponent's king and deliver "checkmate"!

Section 2

Notation 37
Check & Checkmate 39
Special Moves 57
Chess Etiquette 65
Games Ending in a Draw 67

36

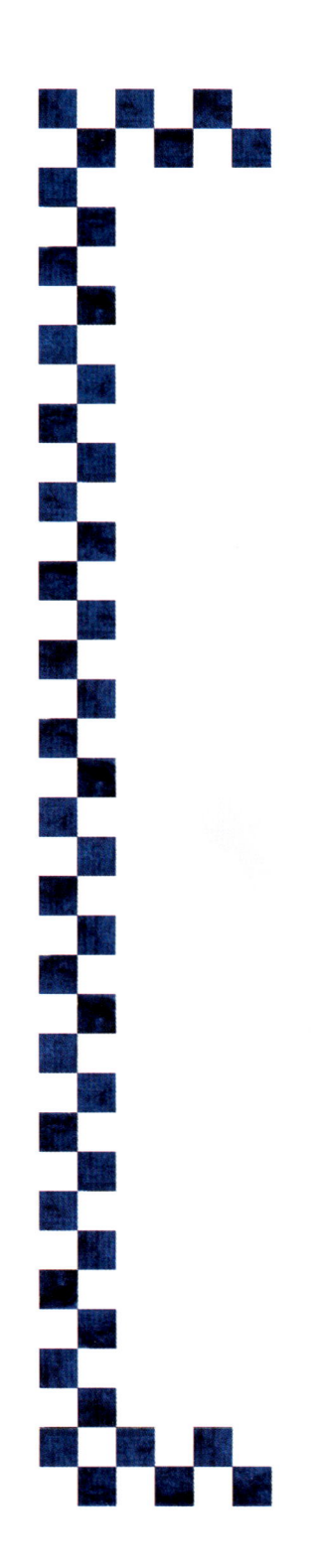

5
NOTATION

Why is notation useful?

Chess notation enables you to go through the games and problems in this book.
It is also essential if you wish to study your games with another chess player.
It is important if you wish to participate in tournaments.
It is certainly a good idea to learn to write down your moves.

Notation

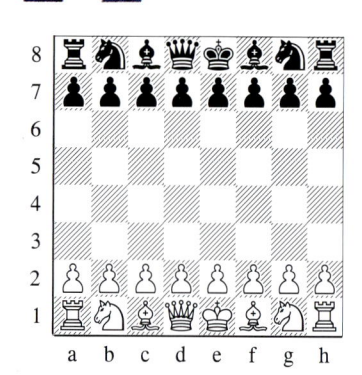

On the chess board you will see that there are numbers **1** to **8** on the left and letters **a** to **h** on the bottom of the board. We use one letter and one number for each square.
For example: **a1** is the square on the bottom left.
It is quite easy to notate or write the moves.

Write a capital letter for each piece:
K: King Q: Queen R: Rook B: Bishop N: Knight.
Note that there is no letter for the pawn.

Take notice of two things here:
1. There is no letter for the pawn, chess players don't use any;
2. Use "K" for the king and "N" for the knight.

If there is no capital letter written then it is a pawn move.
For example, **e4** is a pawn move.
> (The pawn on the "e" file is moving to the **e4** square)
> The pawn could be on **e2** or **e3** before moving to **e4**.

You are nearly ready to begin notating games.

The white king begins on **e1**. The black rooks begin on **a8** and **h8**. If we begin a game where the pawn in front of the king moves two squares forward, we write **e2-e4**, or easier again **e4**. For a move in which the knight moves from **g1** to **f3**, we write **g1-f3** or **N-f3**.
Write "**x**" when a piece is captured. For example, **Nxe4** means that the knight moves and captures whatever piece is on **e4**.

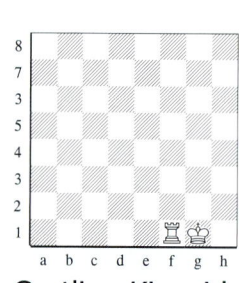

Here are a few extra notes:

x	**Capturing**
O-O	**Castling kingside**
O-O-O	**Castling queenside**
+	**Check**
++ or #	**Checkmate**
!	**Good move**
?	**Bad move**
??	**Whoops a Daisy! Very bad move.**

Castling Kingside.
O-O

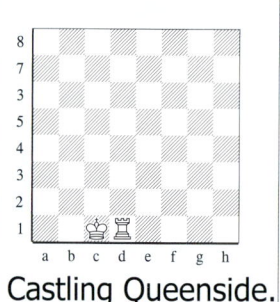

Castling Queenside.
O-O-O

6
CHECK & CHECKMATE
At last, the deadly checkmate!

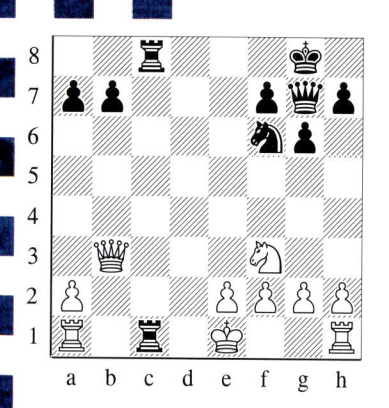

Check & Checkmate

This example is similar to the one you encountered on page 17 when you first learned about **"CHECK"**. In the diagram on the left the **black rook** on c1 is attacking the **white king** on e1. You now know that the term for this attack on the king is **"CHECK"**. It's not absolutely necessary to say but it's no harm to say "check" to your opponent. If the king is in **check** it must be moved from the attacking position immediately. If the king cannot escape from **CHECK**, this is **CHECKMATE** and the game is over, the winner is the player who has delivered **CHECKMATE**.

If you are in check you **must** move out of check **immediately**.

There are three ways to safely get out of check:

3 WAYS TO ESCAPE FROM CHECK: Move - Capture - Block
1. Move the king to a safe square (**Move**): - the king can move to d2.
2. Capture the attacker (**Capture**): - the white rook on a1 can kill or capture the black rook on c1.
3. Move a piece between the enemy attacker and the king (**Block**):
    - the queen can move to d1 and block the check.

What is the best move?
1. **Move:** In moving the king, you are placing him out in an open where he becomes vulnerable to attack from the two black rooks working together. Do you remember how the king is best in hiding most of the time? Except for the endgame after queens have been captured.
2. **Capture:** The white rook on a1 can capture the black rook on c1. The black rook on c8 can recapture and put the king into check again where the king then has no option but to move to d2 or block the check with queen-d1 (and we don't want to loose the queen). If you move the king (after the rook exchange) to d2, there'll be a nice meal for the black rook on h1. Can you see how it would safely capture the rook on h1 and win a piece.
3. **Block:** If you place the queen on d1 you'll be losing a very powerful piece for a rook. Do you remember the value of the pieces? Queen - nine points; Rook - five points.

Everything seems dreadful. What is the best move from such an awful choice?
It is difficult to decide the best escape for White but at least White does not lose any material on moving the king, i.e. K-d2. However there is further mayhem when black's knight enters the attack with a check on e4. The black queen can then enter into the battle. It may be unwise to venture into this attack. If White decides to opt for option 2 and swap the queen for the rook, White will enter the endgame with an extra rook and a clear advantage.

Checkmate

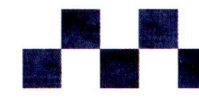

If your KING cannot escape from CHECK to a safe position, this is CHECKMATE and the end of the game.

Look at the diagram on the right.
The **white rook** on d8 is attacking the **black king** on g8.
The king cannot escape from the attack.
This is checkmate and the end of the game.
White has won.

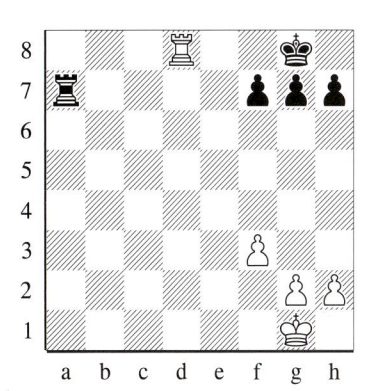

Some Checkmates...

In order to get checkmate on your opponent who has no more than a king left, you must have at least the following pieces along with your KING:
1. **Queen** or
2. **Rook** or
3. **Two Bishops** or
4. **Bishop and Knight** or
5. **Three Knights.**

Clearly, if you have more material the struggle is even easier!

Opposite a KING **you cannot deliver checkmate** if all you have on the board is:
1. A **King and Bishop** or
2. A **King and Knight** or
3. A **King and two Knights.**

If you have a pawn, you cannot deliver checkmate with the pawn alone but you can change it to a queen or a rook when it reaches the final rank ("Pawn Promotion", page 60) and then deliver checkmate.

On the following pages you will learn the most straightforward methods for delivering checkmate with the queen and rook.

...Some Common Checkmates
TWO ROOKS AND KING OPPOSITE A KING

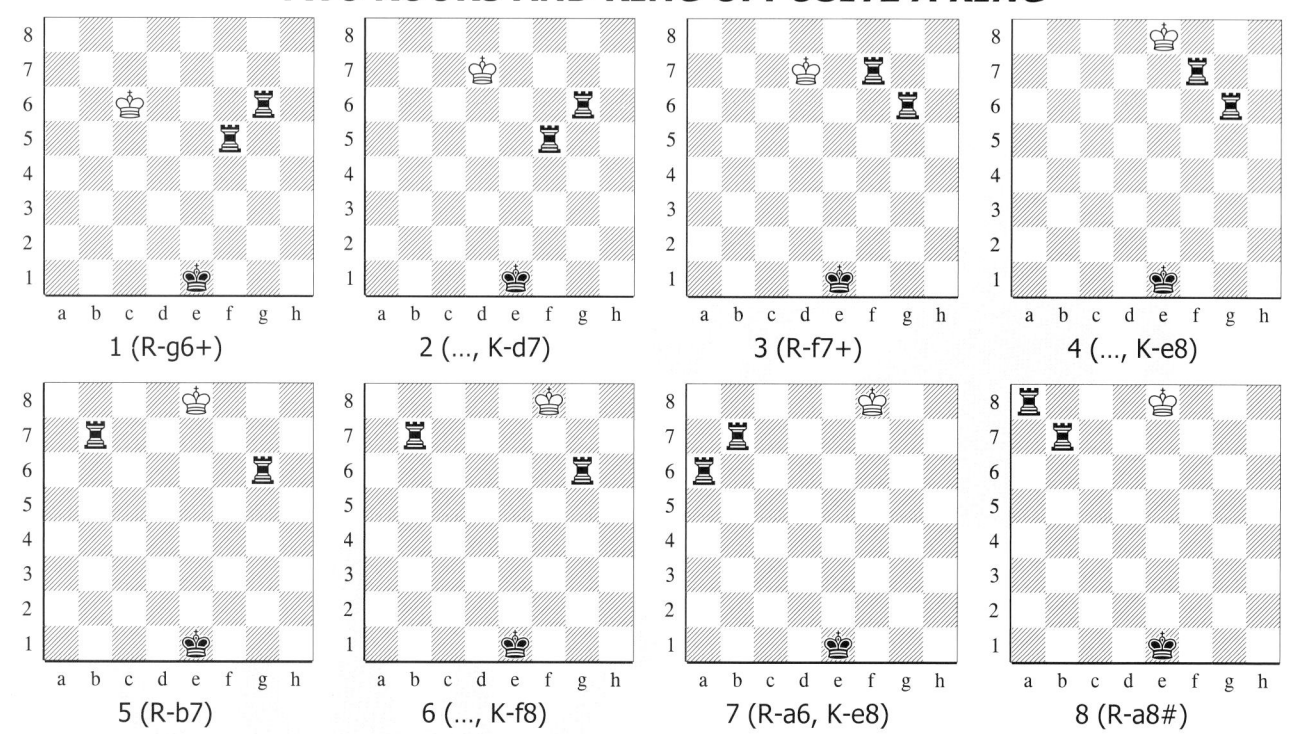

| 1 (R-g6+) | 2 (..., K-d7) | 3 (R-f7+) | 4 (..., K-e8) |
| 5 (R-b7) | 6 (..., K-f8) | 7 (R-a6, K-e8) | 8 (R-a8#) |

1. **B** **R-g6+**: The WHITE KING is in check. He must move immediately out of check.
2. **W** **K-d7**: The WHITE KING must move out of check. Ranks 5 and 6 are controlled by the BLACK ROOK. This means that the KING must move to the 7th rank, in the direction of the ROOKS in a slow effort to perhaps make an attack on a rooks. The poor KING moves so slowly, ...but maybe! Never give up! You never know, your opponent might just blunder.
3. **B** **R-f7+**: The BLACK ROOK checks the KING again, now controlling the 7th rank while the other rook controls the 6th rank.
4. **W** **K-e8**: At last, the KING is able to attack the ROOK.
5. **B** **R-b7**: Ah! The ROOK is too clever for him. This is too easy! RUN! ESCAPE! The ROOK still controls the squares on the 7th rank.
6. **W** **K-f8;** :The tired old KING tries to move in the direction of the ROOK.
7. **B** **R-a6**: The WHITE KING is attacking the g8 square. Black would like to move the ROOK on g6 to the g8 square but it's not safe. Ah well! He can also RUN! **- R-a6.**
8. **W** **K-e8:** The weary KING tries to move in the direction of the ROOKS again!
9. **B** **R-a8#**: The BLACK ROOK moves to a8 and at last delivers the deadly **checkmate!**

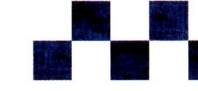

...Some common Checkmates
QUEEN, ROOK AND KING AGAINST A KING

1. The WHITE KING is in check. He must immediately move out of check.
2. He moves to the 7th rank and in the direction of the rook in a slow effort to attack the rook, but the king's legs are not so fast. But maybe!
3. The BLACK ROOK attacks the KING with check.
4. I don't believe that the KING can make a realistic attack on this occasion. He moves to e8 but the BLACK QUEEN is just too powerful - the queen protects the rook from capture
5. Q-g8# and **checkmate!**

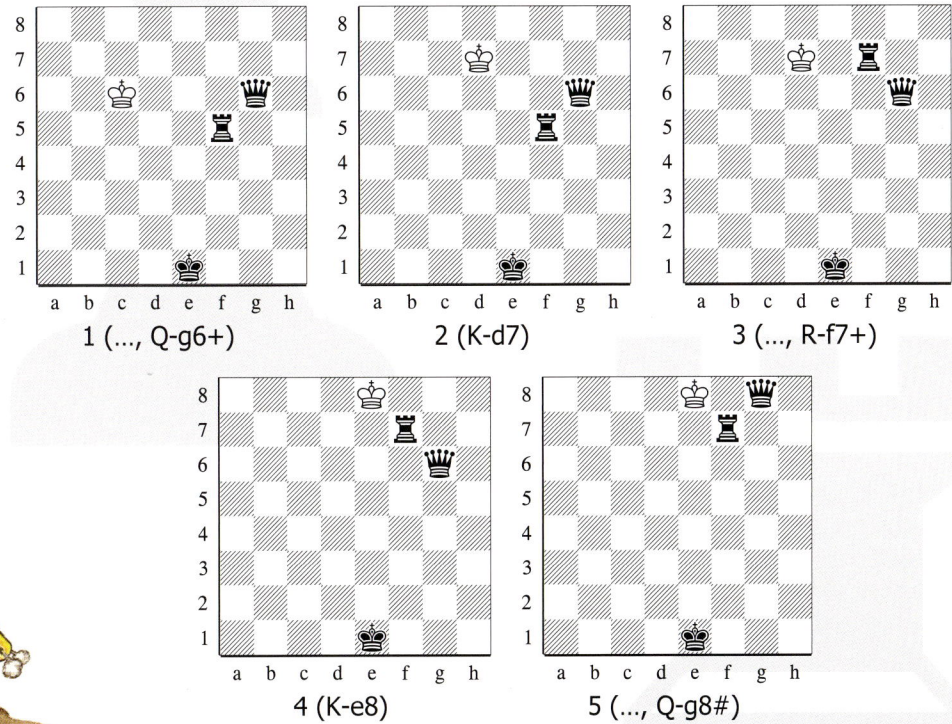

1 (..., Q-g6+)   2 (K-d7)   3 (..., R-f7+)

4 (K-e8)   5 (..., Q-g8#)

Ideas at the end of a game are usually similar to this example: **Chase the KING into a corner or to the side of the board where it has less mobility - then find CHECKMATE!**

Control the squares in front of the enemy king to reduce mobility.

...Some common Checkmates
ROOK AND KING OPPOSITE A KING

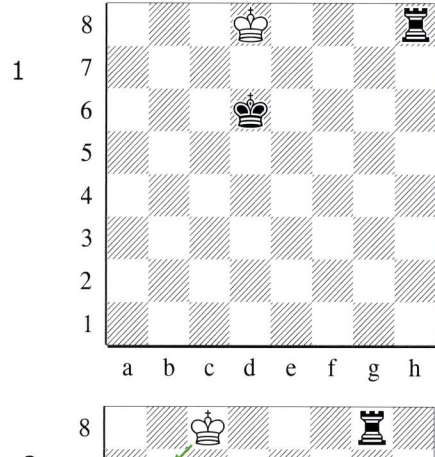

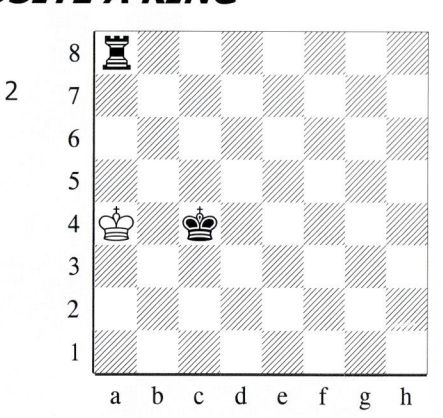

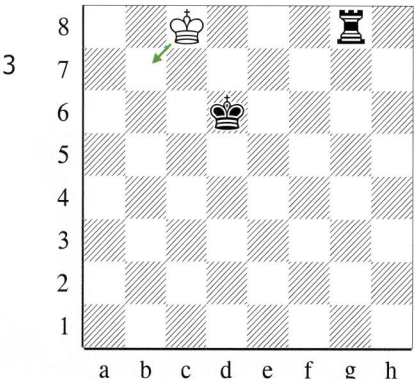

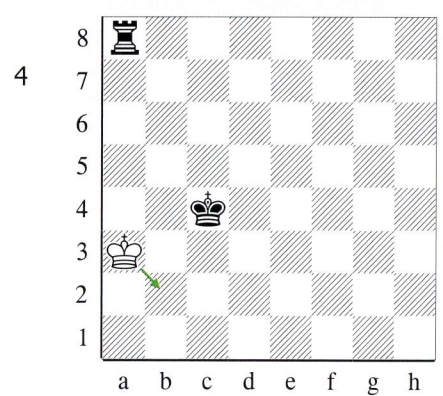

1. Diagrams 1 and 2: This is the final position when you deliver CHECKMATE with a ROOK and a KING. As you can see it's important the KING and ROOK are working together as a team.
2. Take note that the **KINGS are directly opposite each other**. You must wait until your opponent moves his / her KING directly opposite yours before you move your rook to the last rank (Diagram 1) or file (Diagram 2). On this occasion it is the black king that controls the squares in front of the white king.
3. In Diagrams 3 and 4, the KINGS are not directly opposite each other. Therefore, White's king is able to escape.

> **Control the squares in front of the enemy king**
> with your rook or king, to reduce mobility.

...Some common Checkmates
QUEEN AND KING OPPOSITE A KING

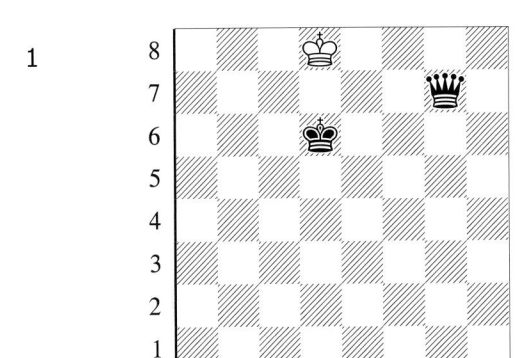

1

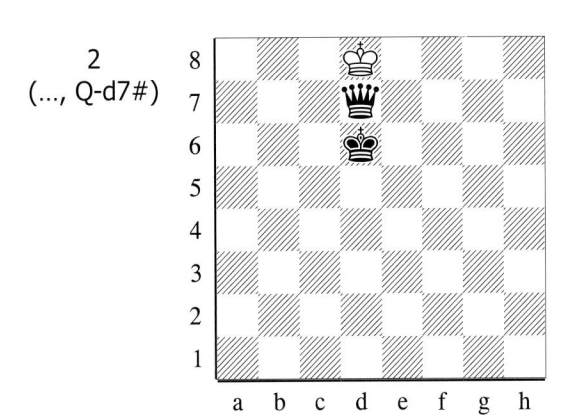

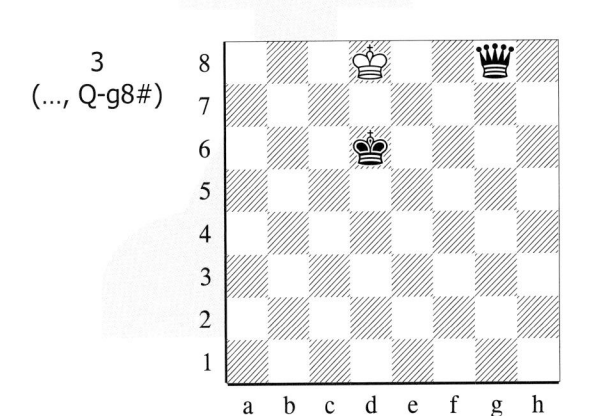

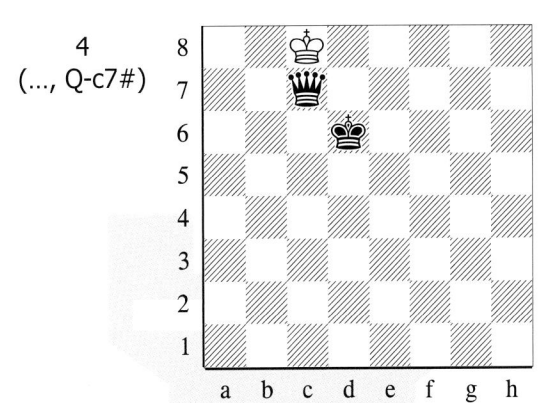

2 (..., Q-d7#)

3 (..., Q-g8#)

4 (..., Q-c7#)

1. Diagram 1: Nearly checkmate! The BLACK KING is important in delivering CHECKMATE. It is important that the KING and QUEEN join forces and work together. In this position Black has a choice of CHECKMATES.
2. Here the BLACK QUEEN delivers checkmate on d7.
3. Another way to deliver CHECKMATE is Q-g8# (Diagram 3).
4. In diagram 4 see how it is not necessary for the KINGS to be directly opposite each other to deliver checkmate. In the endgame with the ROOK and KING opposite a lone KING, the kings must be opposite each other to deliver checkmate.

...Some common Checkmates

KNIGHT, QUEEN AND KING OPPOSITE A KING

Diagram 1 and 2:
Checkmates with
KNIGHT, QUEEN and KING.

In this case, the KING does not have to play a starring role to deliver checkmate. Nevertheless it is always an advantage for the KING to be at work in the endgame.

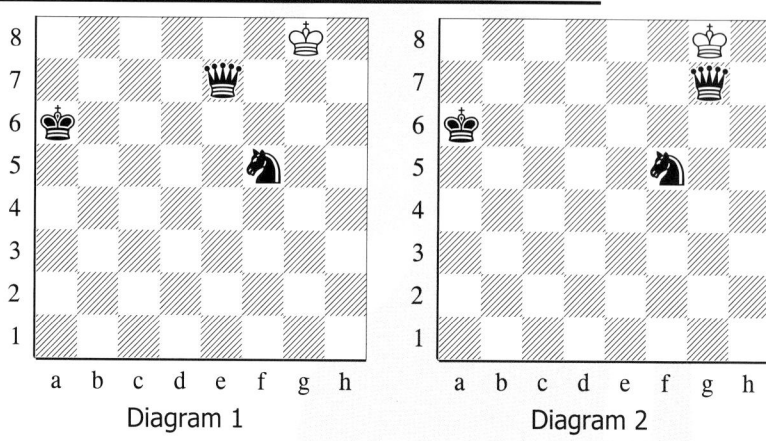

Diagram 1

Diagram 2

BISHOP, QUEEN AND KING OPPOSITE A KING

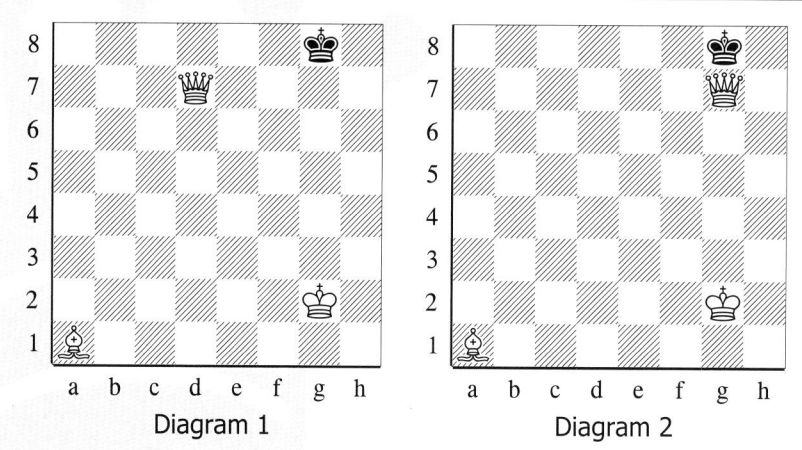

Diagram 1

Diagram 2

Diagram 1 and 2:
Here we see checkmate with a BISHOP and a QUEEN. In this case, the KING can leave the battle to his comrades. Try to chase the KING into a corner with the same coloured square as your BISHOP. The long range of the BISHOP delivers a quick result. As before it's no harm to get the KING into the thick of the battle in the endgame.

Lesson 9
Checkmate Puzzles

Study the following diagrams. Can you see checkmate in one move?
Answers in Chapter 19 - "Puzzles & Lessons: ANSWERS"; now, no cheating!

Always take note of piece mobility.

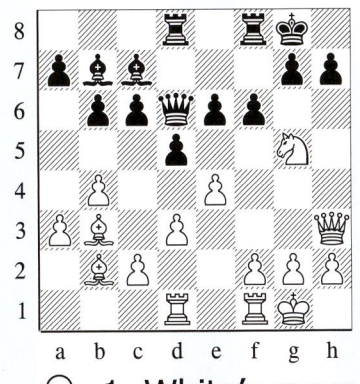

○ 1. White's move

Answer:

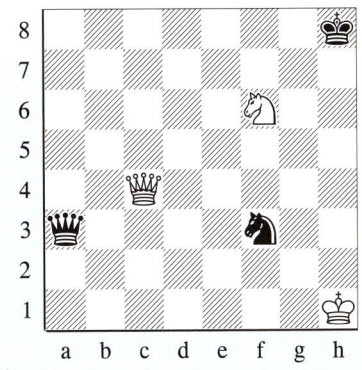

○ 2. White's move

Answer:

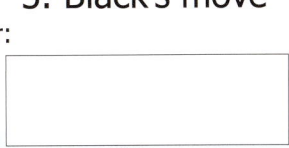

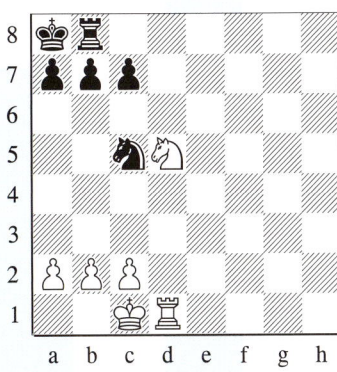

○ 3. White's move

Answer:

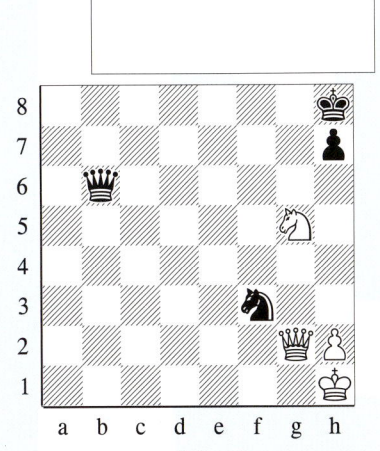

○ 4. White's move

Answer:

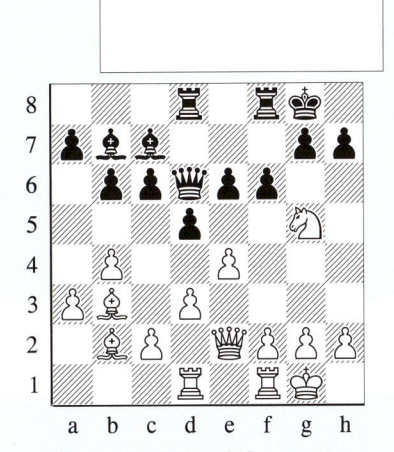

● 5. Black's move

Answer:

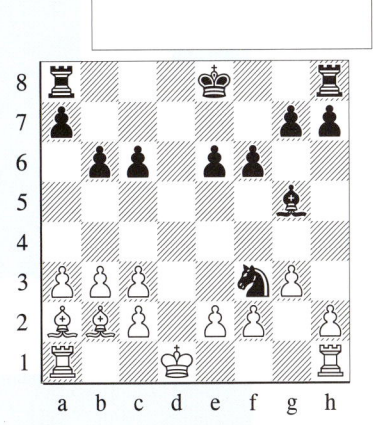

● 6. Black's move

Answer:

Checkmate Puzzles...

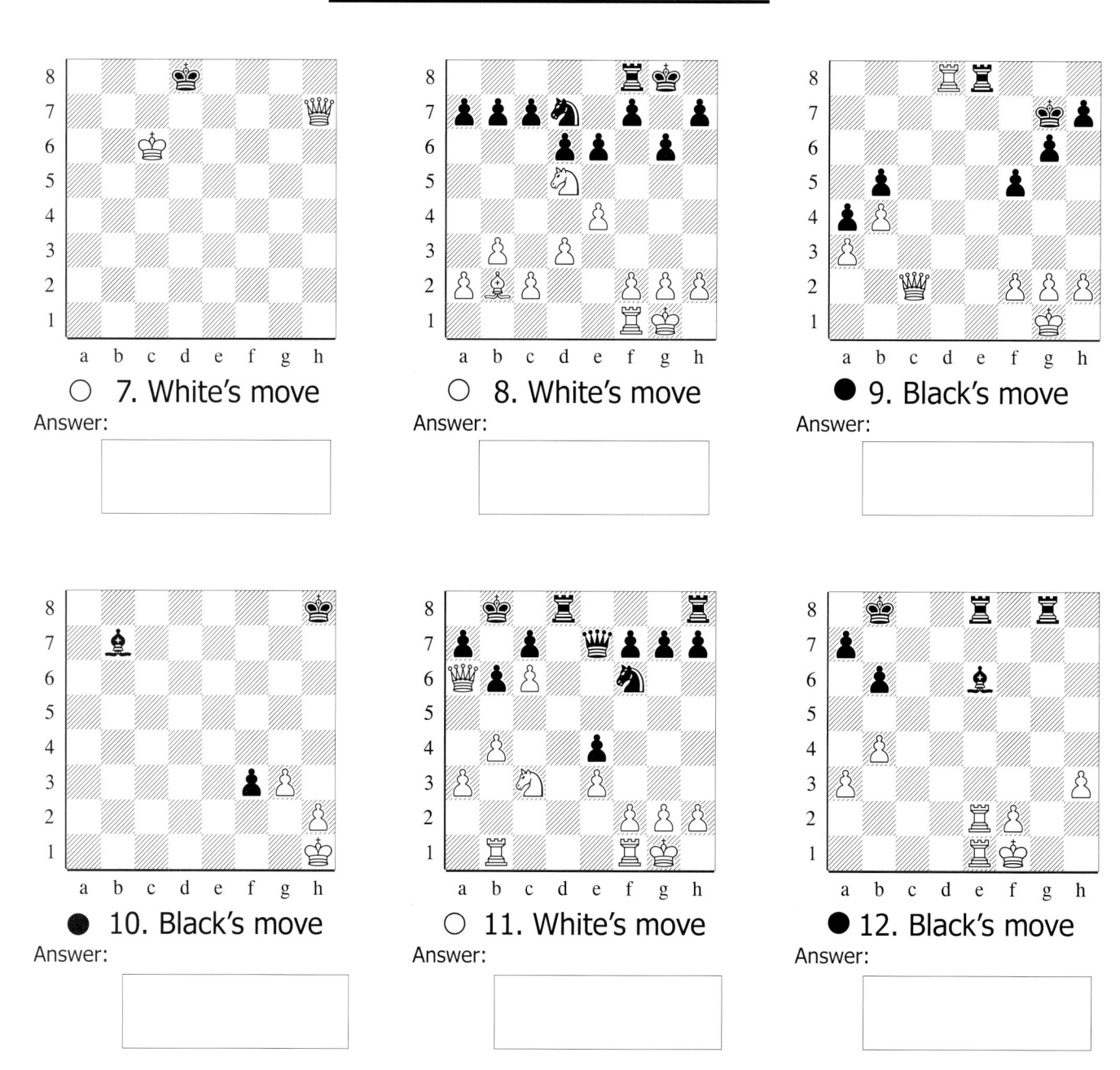

○ **7. White's move**

Answer:

○ **8. White's move**

Answer:

● **9. Black's move**

Answer:

● **10. Black's move**

Answer:

○ **11. White's move**

Answer:

● **12. Black's move**

Answer:

In the following diagrams find the checkmate in TWO moves,

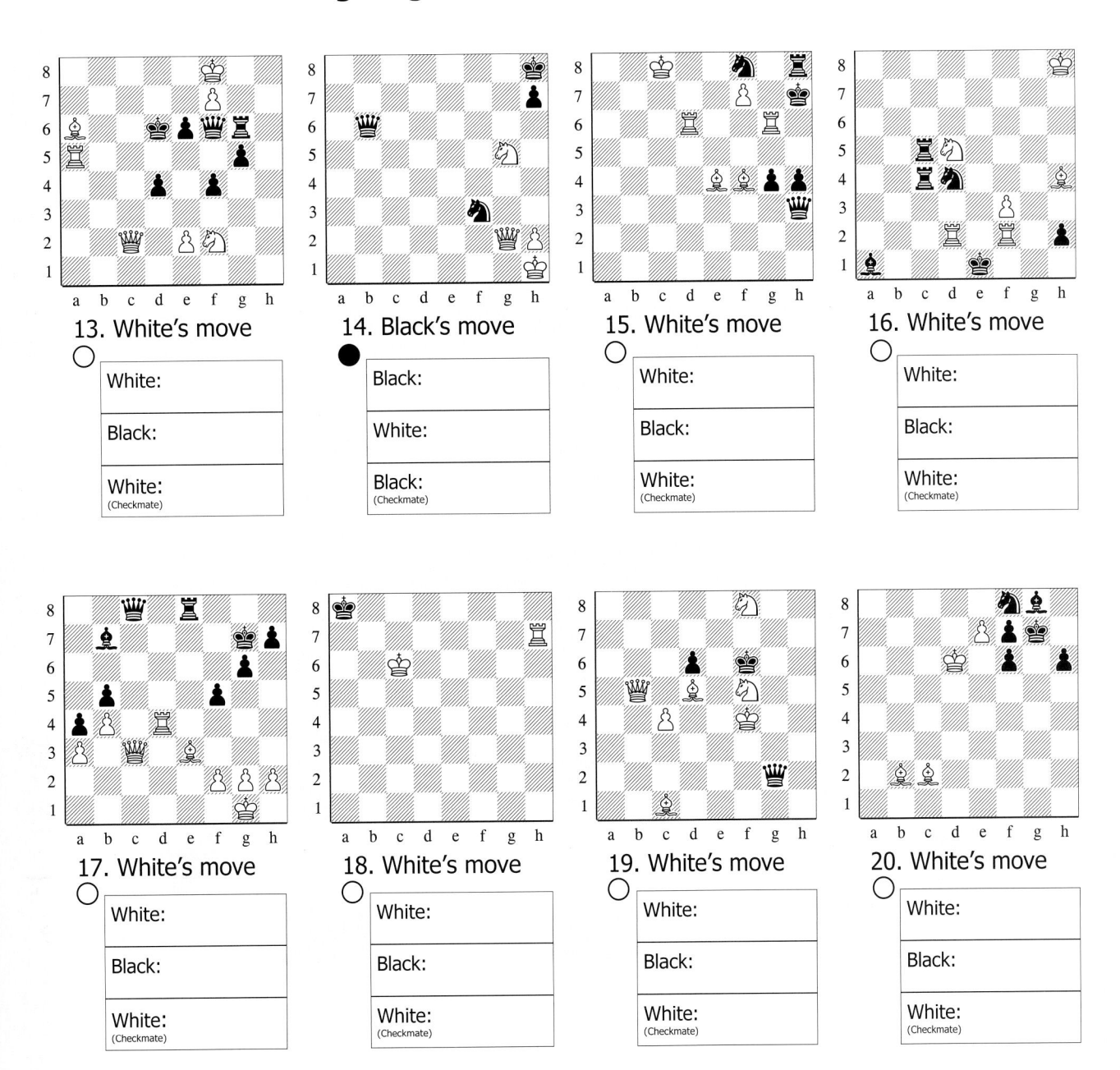

13. White's move

White:
Black:
White: (Checkmate)

14. Black's move

Black:
White:
Black: (Checkmate)

15. White's move

White:
Black:
White: (Checkmate)

16. White's move

White:
Black:
White: (Checkmate)

17. White's move

White:
Black:
White: (Checkmate)

18. White's move

White:
Black:
White: (Checkmate)

19. White's move

White:
Black:
White: (Checkmate)

20. White's move

White:
Black:
White: (Checkmate)

Quick Checkmate

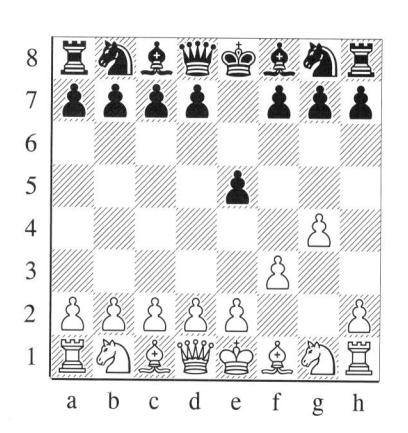

Black	= player with black pieces
black	= black piece
White	= player with white pieces
white	= white piece
1.xxx	= white's move
1… xxx	= black's move

Fool's Mate

This is the fastest checkmate in chess.
White begins.

1.   f3   e5
2.   g4, - whoops!

… Can you see the checkmate?

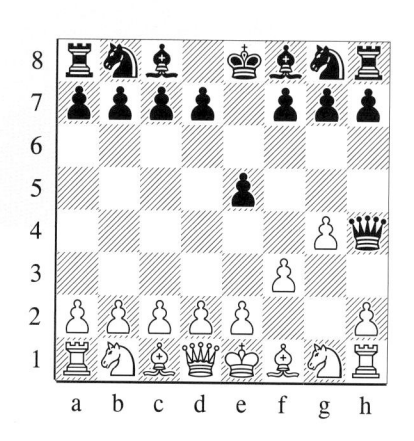

2.   …   Q-h4#, checkmate!

Why White loses so quickly…

1. Moving pawns in front of the king at the beginning of the game is dangerous.
2. Remember that pawns don't move backwards.
3. If the pawns are moved too early to expose the king this creates chances for the opponent to attack the king.

Make sure this doesn't happen to you…

1. Don't make too many pawn moves at the beginning of a game.
2. Be especially careful of pawn moves that expose your king.

...Quick Checkmate

Here is another quick checkmate:
Scholar's Mate

As usual White begins.
1. e4   e5
2. B-c4   N-c6
3. Q-f3   B-c5??

Blunder! A big mistake from Black!

... Can you see the checkmate?

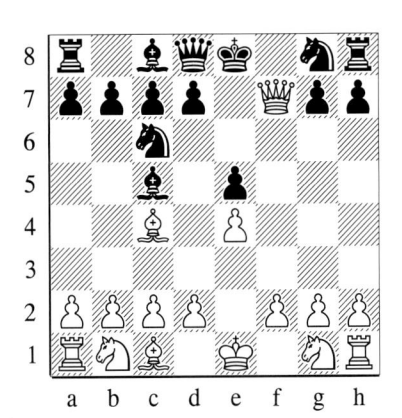

4.   Qxf7#, checkmate!

Why Black loses so quickly...

1. f7 is the magic square. It is a weak square as only the king is protecting it.
2. White got out the troops with a keen eye on the weak f7 pawn. Always watch weak squares.
3. Black thinks about developing, which is good, but forgets to consider each and every move from White.
4. Remember if your opponent can attack that f7 square twice, one of the pieces being the queen, then checkmate may be imminent.

Make sure this doesn't happen to you...

1. Before castling, f7 is the square to keep an eye on.
2. Block White's access to the f7 square by moving the knight to f6.

...Quick Checkmate

Ideas on preventing your opponent from getting **Scholar's Mate**

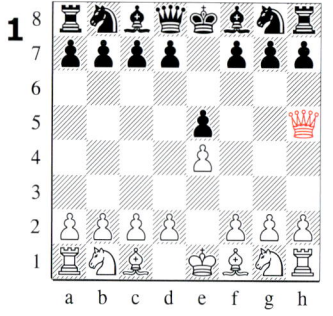

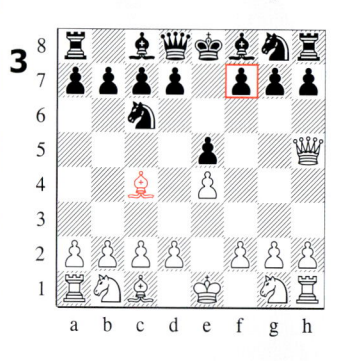

1. e4, e5; Q-h5

Here is how Scholar's Mate may begin. White's queen has a hungry eye on the f7 pawn and on the e5 pawn. At least the king is looking after the f7 pawn so let's deal with the e5 pawn for now. Know that when the white queen comes out like that there may be trouble on its way but not the kind of trouble that's going to frighten you! Let's protect the e5 pawn and develop a piece. What do you think?

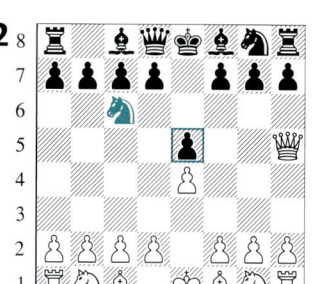

2. Black: N-c6

This looks like a good response!

3. White: B-c4

Now the demon bishop advances to c4 so there are two pieces attacking the f7 pawn and only the king defending it. At least the e5 pawn is safe. What should Black do?

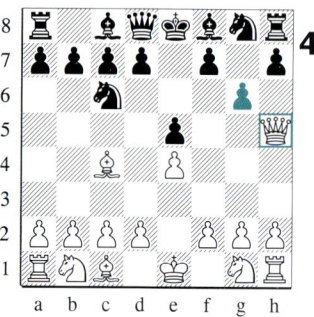

4. Black: g6

That I like! The pawn attacks the queen while blocking the dangerous diagonal of the queen.

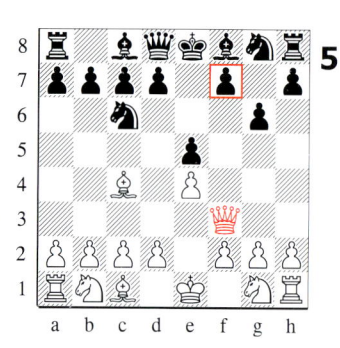

5. White: Q-f3

The queen retreats to f3 and threatens mate on f7 again.

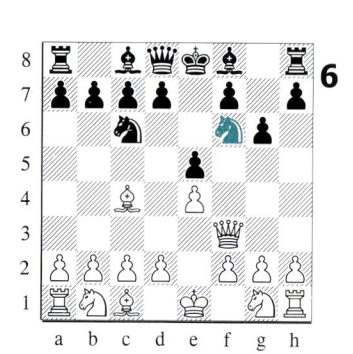

6. Black: N-f6

Don't worry! Let's develop our g8 knight and block the checkmate on f7. See how the knight is protected by the queen and soon the bishop on f8 may come out to g7 to protect it further and leave the queen free to work.

...Quick Checkmate

Ideas on preventing your opponent from getting **Scholar's Mate**

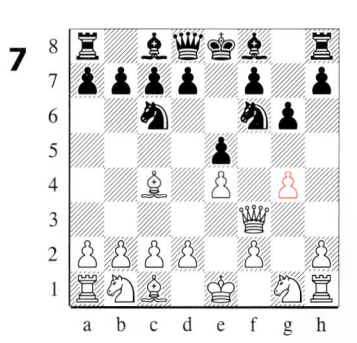

7. White: g4
White has ideas of following this up with g5 to drive the f6 knight away so mating plans may be on track again.

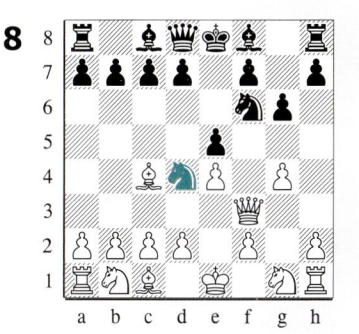

8. Black: N-d4
Wow! There's a very powerful knight in the centre of the board. This knight is no longer required to protect the e5 pawn and so sets about on another mission. Let's attack the queen! It appears that the knight is also attacking the c2 pawn. This looks very strong for Black, could White possibly have a response?

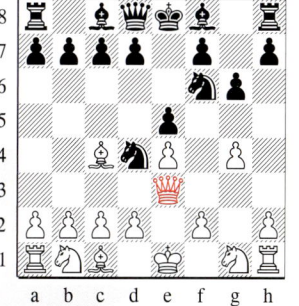

9. White: Q-e3
The g4 pawn has no time to advance to chase the black knight on f6, the queen must be looked after first. What if the queen moves to e3?

Black: I'm thinking there's a delicious meal for Black somewhere. Can you find it?

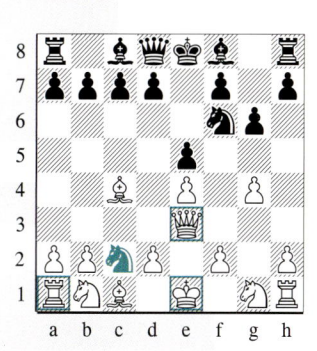

The knight was also attacking the unprotected c2 pawn when it attacked the queen. A knight in the centre is a very powerful thing. Now Black moves in and captures the c-pawn while forking the king, queen and rook. The king must first move out of check giving no time to save the queen. The white queen is clearly lost. White took out the queen too early and has paid dearly for the early attack without fully developing pieces.

...Quick Checkmate

Ideas on preventing your opponent from getting **Scholar's Mate**

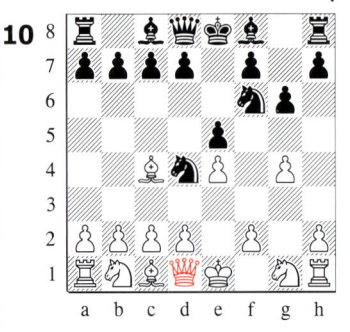

10. White: Q-d1
Let's say White doesn't move the **queen** to c3 but decides to go back home instead to **d1**, what are Black's options now?

11. Black: Nxe4
It looks like the e4 pawn is now unprotected and a free meal is on offer! And another powerful **knight** in the centre. This looks like a lot of fun for Black!

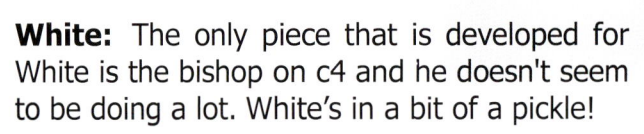

White: The only piece that is developed for White is the bishop on c4 and he doesn't seem to be doing a lot. White's in a bit of a pickle!

Black: Black is happy with those powerful knights in the centre and the queen ready to come out to exploit White's weaknesses created by an overenthusiastic opening. Even if White tries to chase the knight with f3, White's queen just muscles in on h4 with check. There's no escaping mate on f2.

12 & 13. See how Black can exploit White's weaknesses. If White decides to attack the central knight by playing **f3**. Black would now think about mate on **f2** after Q-h4+ where the knight and queen would work together.

14. Some people try to get Scholar's Mate by moving the **queen** to f3. The simplest move for Black is **N-f6**, blocking the queen's path to f7. As long as your knight stays on f6 while the threat exists, you'll be ok.

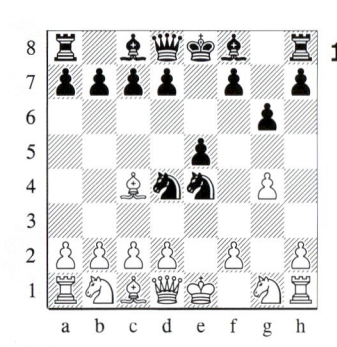

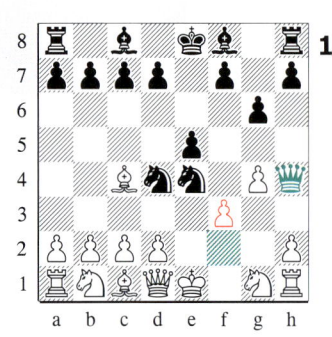

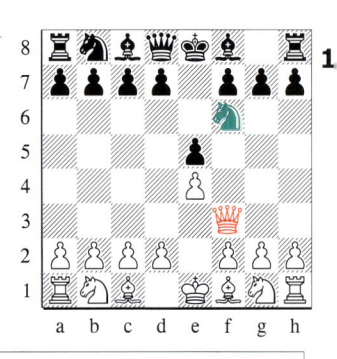

If you try "Scholar's Mate" against someone who doesn't know it, you may win quickly.
If you try "Scholar's Mate" against someone good, you'll probably run into trouble.
If someone tries "Scholar's Mate" against you, look forward to it!

...Quick Checkmate

Reti's Mate

Here is a very clever checkmate from a famous chess master called **Richard Reti.**

Reti: White.

1. There are eight moves already made up to now and then a lightening inspiration hit Reti!

Do you see the checkmate?

2. Reti begins with a brilliant queen sacrifice: **Q-d8+**

3. Black has no choice, Black must capture the queen: **Kxd8**

4. White unleashes a double check from White: **B-g5+**

   (from the g5 bishop and the d1 rook)

5. Black must move the king to c7: **K-c7** (If ...K-e8 then R-d8#)

............can you see what happened next?

6. B-d8#, checkmate!

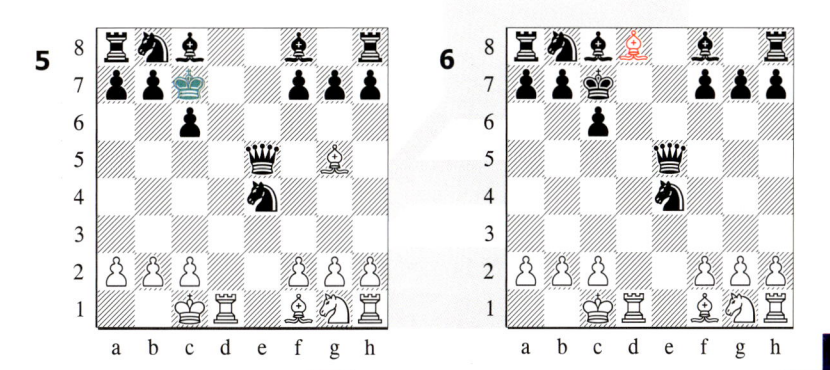

...Quick Checkmate
Legall's Checkmate

(from the French chess master: Legall De Kermeur (1702-1792),

1. **e4   e5,**
2. **N-f3   d6,**
3. **N-c3   B-g4,** (Diagram 1)

White has played a good opening up until now, taking out the pieces as quickly as possible. The knights are developed and looking to exert pressure on the centre; that's brilliant.

Knights before bishops, as a wise one once said!

Black, however, has only developed two pawns and one bishop. This is not a complete disaster but Black should consider taking out the knights or he might get into trouble.

4. **B-c4   g6,** (Diagram 2)

White develops a bishop and eyes up the f7 square that is only protected by the black king. Now White has three pieces out in the main battleground and Black has only one. White is correct in developing the pieces as quickly as possible and especially in developing the knights first.

5. **Nxe5** (Diagram 3)

Here, White placed his hand on the knight by mistake. In chess rules: "If you touch a piece you must move that piece" ("Touch Move", page 61). He thought for a bit and then captured the pawn on e5.

5. **...   Bxd1** (yum, yum! Or maybe not!)

Black swoops quickly and grabs the unfortunate white queen. Black doesn't think at all here. Moving without thinking can be a fatal mistake in chess, chess players are cute rascals!!!

Black ate up the queen, "nice yummy meal", he said to himself, without proper thought! Do you see what White has in store?

6. **Bxf7+   K-e7,**

The white bishop captures the pawn on f7 and attacks the black king - check!. Black must move his king into safety immediately. The black king only has one option, the king must move to e7.

7. **N-d5#, checkmate!** Nice! (Diagram 4)

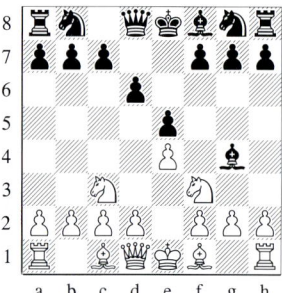

Diagram 1 (N-c3, B-g4)

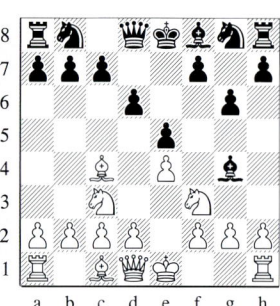

Diagram 2 (B-c4, g6)

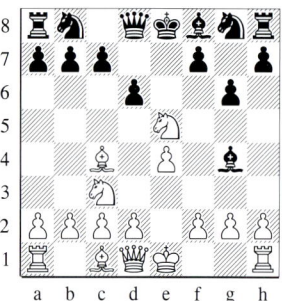

Diagram 3 (Nxe5, Bxd1)

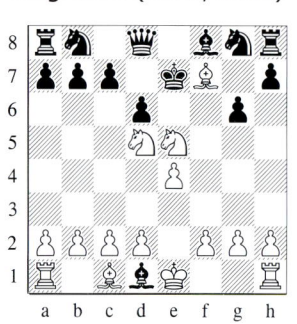

Diagram 4
(Bxf7+, K-e7; N-d5#)

7
SPECIAL MOVES

It is now time to learn all of the special moves in chess!

Castling

Castling is a special move in which two pieces, the king and the rook, move at the same time. You can only make this move once in any game.

Why castle? Good question!

Often it is a good idea to put the king into hiding behind pawns. Castling also connects your rooks and enables them to play in the centre. More importantly, it gets your king into a safe place. After you have castled, your king is easier to defend against enemy threats. If you leave your king in the centre he can be attacked from all directions.

This is the only time that the king is allowed to move two squares.

The king moves two squares in the direction of one of the rooks and the rook then hops over him to the square right beside him. As simple as that!

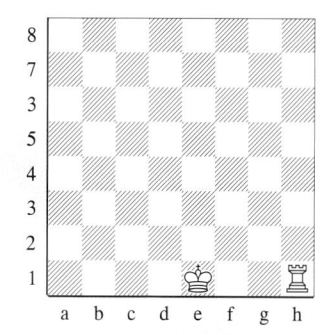

Before castling on the Kingside

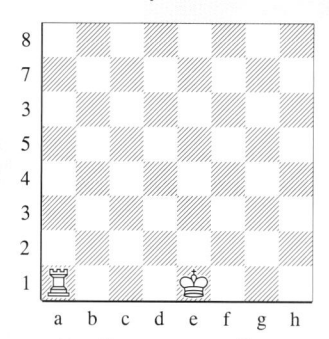

Before castling on the Queenside

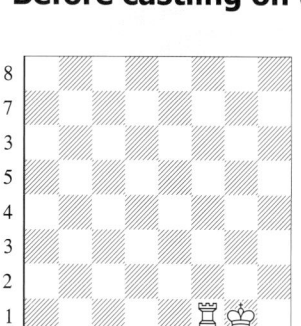

After castling on the Kingside

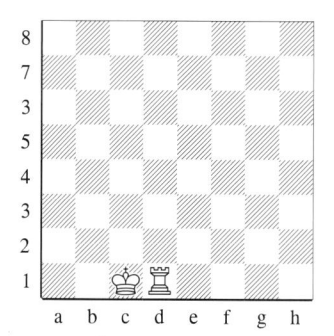

After castling on the Queenside

...Castling

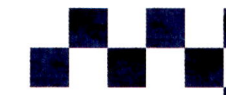

More rules about castling:

Here are a few rules you must take note of if you wish to castle:

- You cannot **castle** if you have previously moved the KING. This is why we recommend blocking checks rather than moving the KING early in the game, if possible.
- You cannot **castle** if you have previously moved the ROOK with which you wish to **castle**.
- You cannot **castle** if you are in CHECK.
- You <u>can</u> **castle** if your ROOK is being attacked.
- While **castling**, the KING cannot pass through a square which an enemy piece is attacking = you cannot move **through** check.
- While **castling**, the KING cannot enter a square that is under attack by an enemy piece. You cannot ever move **into** check.
- You cannot **castle** if there is any piece between the KING and the ROOK.

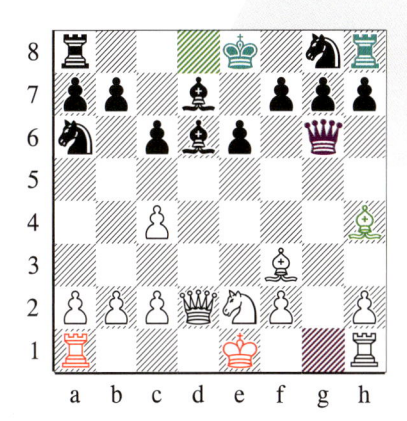

Look at the diagram on the left:

- ■ · White cannot castle on the kingside as he/she would be moving into check from the black queen on g6.
- ■ · White can castle on the queenside.
- ■ · Black cannot castle on the queenside as he/she would be passing through check from the bishop on h4.
- ■ · Black can castle kingside after the knight has been moved out.

Often, learners or beginners think that you cannot castle if you have been in check previously in the game.; this is not true. If you have not moved your KING or your ROOK then you still have the option to castle.

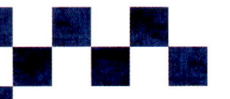

Pawn Promotion

When a pawn succeeds in negotiating enemy territory and lands on the final rank you may change the pawn into whatever piece you wish. It cannot remain as a pawn, you must change it. Usually the pawn is transformed into a queen as she is the most powerful piece in chess. You can also, however, change it to a knight, a bishop or a rook.

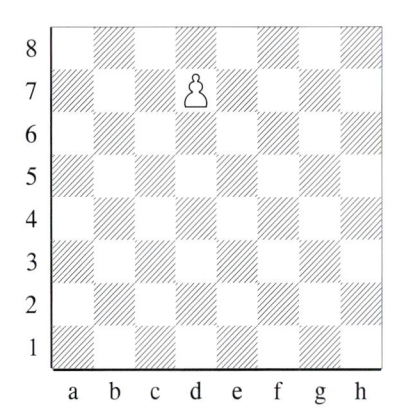

Here is a pawn on d7 hoping be promoted.

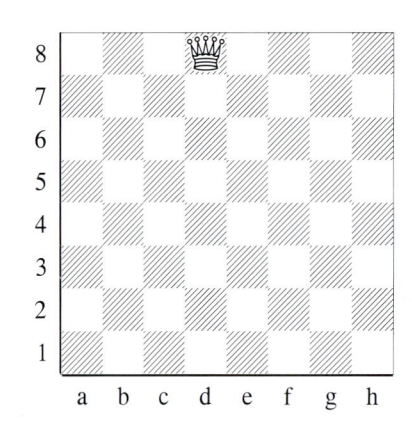

The pawn moves to the final rank and converts to a queen (or a knight, bishop or rook) and remains in the same square. The pawn is removed from the game.

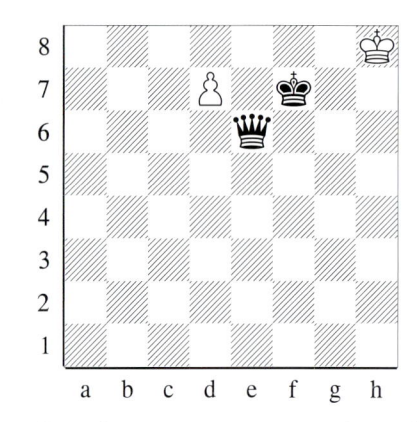

If White promotes the d7 pawn to a queen, White loses after Q-h6# (checkmate). However if White promotes the pawn to a knight, this creates a fork on the king and queen, thus winning the queen and drawing the game.

d8 (Knight), K-f6 or e7; Nxe6, Kxe6. With only kings left on the board the game is declared a draw.

An extra pawn on your team can be the winning of the game. Always remember that the extra pawn could transform to a queen and give you extra vital power. Always be careful to defend well if your opponent has the extra pawn.

You can have **LOTS OF QUEENS** on the board at the same time. Be really careful! The more queens you have on the board, the more chances you give to your opponent of getting stalemate. See Chapter 9 "Games Ending in a Draw", (page 67) for a full explanation of the "Stalemate" rule.

The rule
"Touch Move"

The "touch move" rule means:

If you touch a piece, you must move it.

If you touch your opponent's piece, you must capture it, if possible.

If you touch a piece, you must move it. When you have moved a piece and *your hand is removed from the piece,* your move is deemed to be finished or completed and it is then time for your opponent to move. If you place your hand on your opponent's piece you must capture it, if there is a legal way to do so.

It is very important to keep your hands away from your pieces until you are completely certain of your move. If you are in any doubt, consider sitting on your hands! Don't hover over the board, you might touch a piece by accident and - aargh! Lose your precious queen!

And don't forget:

If you see a good move, wait a moment as there may be a better move. Look around the chess board and investigate further before you move.

If you wish to settle a piece in a square correctly without actually moving it, you must first say the word *"j'adoube".* This means "I adjust" in French. You may also say "I adjust" or "adjusting". It is important that your opponent knows that you are adjusting the piece correctly in its square and are not about to move it.

"J'adoube" = I adjust

If you see a good move, take a moment;
there's probably a better one there somewhere, try to find a better move!
Never touch a piece until you are absolutely certain you are going to move it!

Capturing a Pawn
"En Passant"

En passant (from the French: "in passing" [the pawn])
The name "en passant" is given to a special type of capture. In this capture a pawn can capture an enemy pawn under specific rules. Here's how it works:

In Diagram 1, it is Black's move. The d-pawn can move one or two squares forward as it has not yet moved. If Black moves d7-d5 the pawn is now directly beside the white pawn on White's **fifth rank**. In this case White can diagonally take the black pawn on d5 if he or she wishes. In the rule "en passant" this move must be made immediately after the **d5** move here. In this example if you wish to use the "en passant" rule, you must do so immediately after Black plays d7-d5.

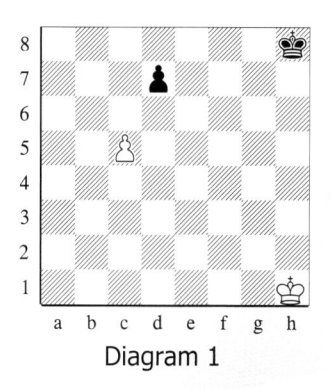

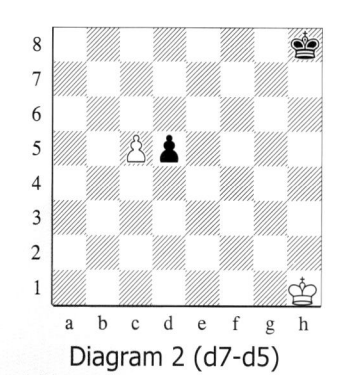

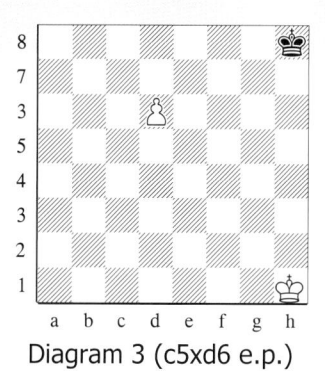

Diagram 1   Diagram 2 (d7-d5)   Diagram 3 (c5xd6 e.p.)

1. You cannot wait for the next turn. If you wish to capture the pawn "en passant", you have to take immediately.
2. The pawns are the only pieces that can capture "en passant".
3. As with any other capture, this move is optional.
4. The move "en passant" can be used many times in a game.

This move is unusual in chess as your piece is moving into a different square than that of the pawn you are capturing.
    In chess notation we write "e.p." for *en passant*.

..."En Passant"

The Rule and the Capture
"En Passant"

1. A player moves the pawn two squares forward, from the second to the fourth rank.
2. The opponent's pawn is sitting right beside the first pawn on it's fifth rank; therefore both pawns are on the same rank, beside each other.
3. The second player may capture the pawn with one move diagonally forward in the next move.
4. The name of this capture is "en passant".
5. Note that you are not moving directly into the square in which the enemy pawn is sitting but the square which it has just passed. The enemy pawn is removed from the game.

When capturing "en passant" you must move **immediately** after your opponent's pawn moves two squares forward to the same rank beside your pawn.

64

8
CHESS ETIQUETTE
Time for chess manners!

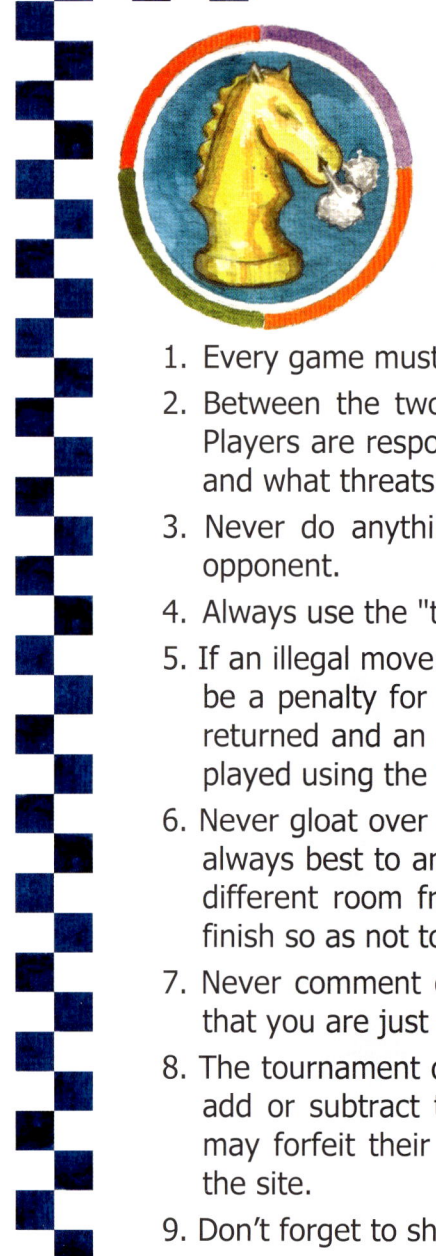

Chess Etiquette

Here are a few important rules of chess etiquette that you should be familiar with, especially when you play your first tournament.

Etiquette: the rules indicating the proper and polite way to behave.

1. Every game must begin and end with the players shaking hands.
2. Between the two handshakes, no talking is permitted. "Check" need not be said. Players are responsible for noticing where all of the pieces on the board are located and what threats are pending.
3. Never do anything to distract any other player in a tournament, especially your opponent.
4. Always use the "touch move" rule.
5. If an illegal move is made, the tournament director should be summoned. There may be a penalty for the player who has delivered the illegal move. The illegal move is returned and an alternative is played. If possible, the original piece moved must be played using the "touch move" rule.
6. Never gloat over a victory, or become despondent or hostile following a defeat. It is always best to analyse the game with your opponent after the game ends, and in a different room from where you played. Leave the playing room quietly when you finish so as not to distract the other people who are still playing.
7. Never comment on a game that is in progress, whether the game is yours or one that you are just watching.
8. The tournament director has the authority to punish breaches of etiquette, and may add or subtract time on the chess clock as a sanction. In extreme cases, players may forfeit their game for violating the rules and spectators may be banned from the site.
9. Don't forget to shake hands after the game; win, lose or draw.

9
GAMES ENDING IN A DRAW

I know! Nobody likes a to draw a game -
we'd all prefer to win!
Let's investigate!

Stalemate

If the king is not in check and he/she cannot move into any square that is free from check and no other piece can make a legal move, this is STALEMATE. This is a DRAWN game. It doesn't matter how many pieces each player has on the board. In the diagrams below it is White's move, but in each case the two pieces that White has left cannot make a legal move. In the first example the only squares available for White's king are controlled by the black knight (g1 and h2) and the black rook (g1 and g2). The white pawn is blocked by the h4 black pawn.
This is **STALEMATE**.

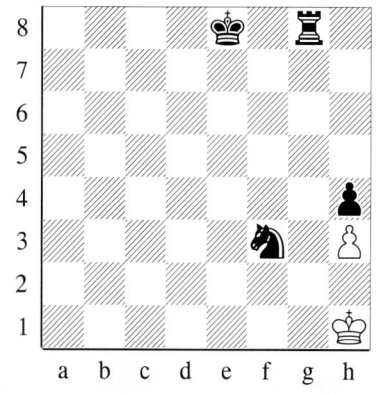

STALEMATE
The game is a draw
White is to play and there is no legal move.

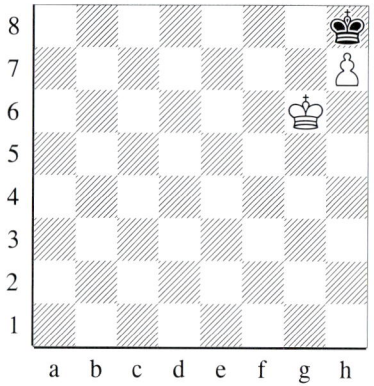

STALEMATE
The game is a draw
Black is to play and there is no legal move.

If a player cannot make a legal move on his / her turn, this is called **STALEMATE**.
- The game is declared a draw and a half point is awarded to each player.

Not Enough Pieces

If there are not enough pieces on the board to checkmate, an end must be put to the game and a draw declared. In the diagram on the right the game is drawn as it is impossible to deliver checkmate with only a KING and KNIGHT.

In order to checkmate your opponent who has only a KING remaining, you must have at least the following combination of pieces to work with your KING:
1. Queen; *or*
2. Rook; *or*
3. Two Bishops; *or*
4. A Bishop and a Knight; *or*
5. Three Knights.

Obviously, the more pieces you have the easier the task!

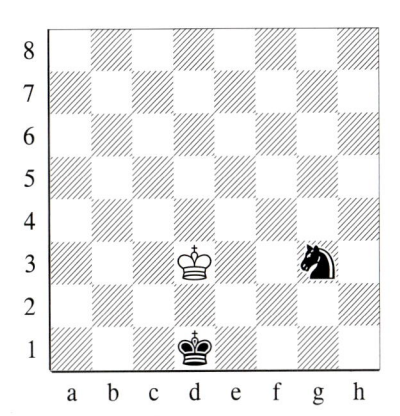

A drawn game
You cannot deliver checkmate with a king and knight alone.

If there are not enough pieces on either side to deliver checkmate, then the score is a draw.
In tournament chess each player gets a half point.

Perpetual Check

A drawn game is declared if the same position appears on the chess board **three times in the game**. This is called **Repetition**. If the same position happens **three times in a row** on the chess board this is called **Threefold Repetition**. If the same position occurs **three times in a row with checks** this is called **Perpetual Check**.

In the position below, White has a lot more material and is much better placed than Black. Nonetheless Black can get a **Perpetual Check**. After three repetitions of the position, it is declared a draw and the end of the game.

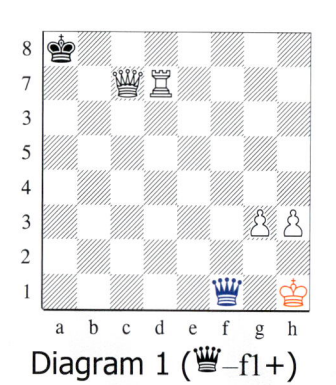

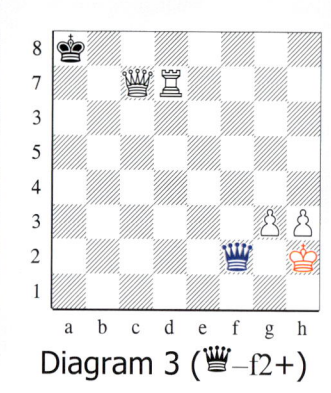

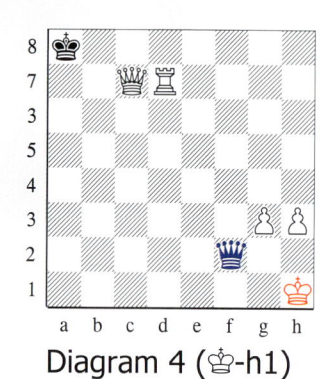

Diagram 1 (♛–f1+)   Diagram 2 (♔–h2)   Diagram 3 (♛–f2+)   Diagram 4 (♔-h1)

1. The black queen moves to f1 and the white king is in check.
2. White must get the king out of check. There is no choice, the king moves to h2.
3. The black queen moves to f2 and the white king is in check again.
4. The white king must move to h1 but White can check again with the position from diagram 1 is repeated.

1. ...., ♛–f1+;
2. ♔-h2, ♛–f2+;
3. ♔-h1, ♛–f1+;
4. ♔-h2, ♛–f2+;
5. ♔-h1, ♛–f1+;
6. ♔-h2   The same position occurs **three times in a row**, this is **Perpetual Check**: the end of the game and a half point to each player.

Threefold repetition

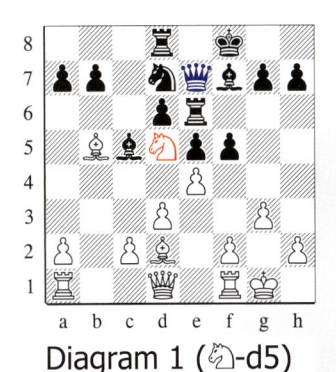

Diagram 1 (♘-d5) 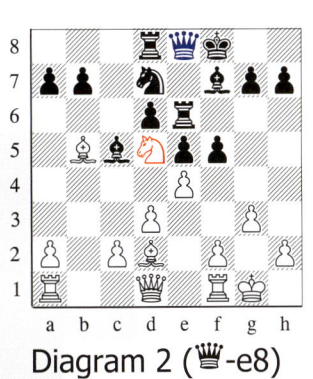 Diagram 2 (♕-e8) 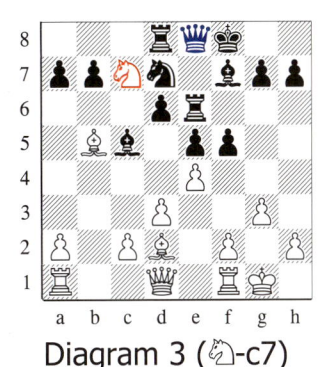 Diagram 3 (♘-c7) 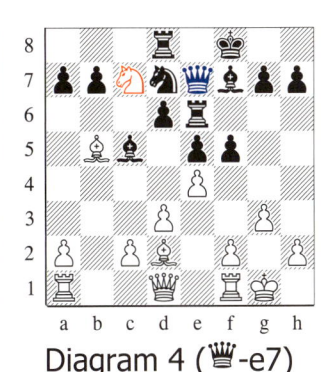 Diagram 4 (♕-e7)

A threefold repetition.
1. ♘-d5 (attacking the queen), ♕-e8 (the only move to save the queen);
2. ♘-c7 (another attack), ♕-e7 (escape again);
3. ♘-d5, ♕-e8;
4. ♘-c7, ♕-e7...etc.

If the same position appears **three times** (not in a row); this is a **threefold repetition**, and a half point to each player.

If the same position appears **three times** in a row; this is **threefold repetition**, and a half point to each player.

50 Move Rule

If a game continues for fifty moves **without a capture or a pawn move** this is a draw.
That is, 50 moves for White and 50 moves for Black.

The diagram on the right illustrates a game with a rook and a bishop opposite a rook. If White can continue the game for 50 moves without a capture, this is a draw.
Note: To count the moves correctly and make your claim you must have your moves notated.

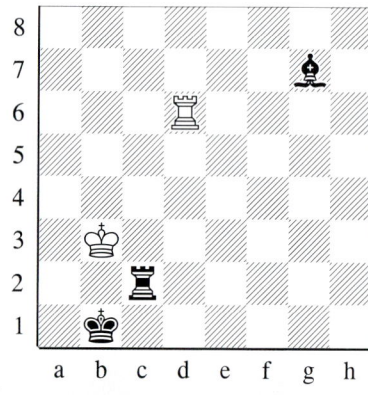

Is this a draw?

If a game continues for 50 moves **without a pawn move or a capture** this is a draw and a half point to each player.

Declaring a Draw

A draw must be declared in the following situations:

1. Stalemate.
2. Not enough material to win.
3. A three-time repetition of position (including perpetual check).
4. Mutual agreement of the players.
5. Fifty moves in a row without a capture or a pawn move.

Section 3

The Opening	**75**
Tactics & Strategy	**81**
The Passed Pawn	**93**
The Greek Gift	**99**
The Endgame	**103**
Chess Players on Different Levels	**105**
A Game from Bobby Fischer	**107**

74

10
THE OPENING

One could write about this subject till the end of time.
There are more books written on Chess Openings
than any other area in the game of chess.
Let's make a start!

The Opening

Now you have all the rules. If you have followed everything up to now, you have enough information to have a good game. Still, if you wish to brush up on your game it's time to think about **Strategy**.
Here we will learn about **Opening Strategies**.
There is more written about the opening of the game of Chess than any other part of the game, perhaps more than any other game anywhere. There are more than nine million positions possible after just three moves. Wow! Do we have to learn all of these off by heart? Definitely not! A lot of professional chess players would learn certain strong Openings off by heart but with a few strategic ideas we can still play the Opening well.

Five Opening Rules

If you decide your opening moves based on the following five rules, you will get off to an excellent start. These rules are relevant to all chess players whether you are a beginner or a grandmaster. They are simple and easy to follow.

Keep in mind that opening play is about gaining a strong position on the board from which to launch your attack, not for embarking on an immediate onslaught.

The MINOR PIECES:
Light Soldiers

Firstly, in the Opening, only move your pawns, knights and bishops (the **MINOR PIECES**). Be careful not to move pawns too much and concentrate more on developing knights and bishops.
Your Minor pieces are good for skirmishes at the beginning of the game and to create a strong position in the centre of the board. The stronger pieces, your queen and rooks (the **MAJOR PIECES**) will be used more later on in the game.

1. Pawns in the Centre

Place one or two pawns in the centre. The centre of the board is where the first power struggle takes place and whoever controls more of the central squares controls the game. Once the pawns have taken up position in the central squares, it's quite hard to dislodge them, so they may stay there for some time.

2. Knights and Bishops in the Centre

This is an important strategy. Bring out your knights and bishops to control the centre. This will mean moving pawns to clear the path for your bishops, which can't jump. Knights, bishops and pawns are your "Light Soldiers" and need to be moved before your queen and rooks (the "Heavy Soldiers"). When starting out it is usually best to bring out knights before bishops.

3. Don't move the same piece twice in the opening
As we have seen, the opening is about putting your pieces into good positions to control the centre and prepare for more work. If you move the same piece around, making attacks, you'll soon end up with only one piece fighting an entire army. Move each piece once in order to give yourself time for your army to come out. Prepare your army, get them working your attacks come later.

4. Guard and Capture
Be careful with the placing of your pieces. If your opponent can capture, make sure you can recapture so the armies stay level. Try to place your pieces so that they are looking after each other while moving pieces out into the battlefield. Bobby Fischer was a master at this.

5. Castle as quickly as possible, usually on the Kingside
Make your king safe by castling early. Castling removes your king from the centre and puts him behind a stockade of pawns protected from enemy attacks. When you are playing you should aim for an opening position like that shown in the diagram on the right.

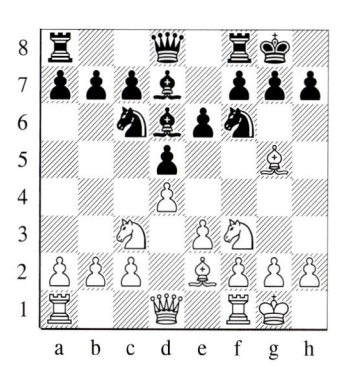

Notes:
1. Both players have pawns in the centre in an effort to control the centre.
2. The minor pieces are out ready for work.
3. Both kings are safe in hiding after castling.
4. All pieces are safe and looking after each other.

---

1. Open with a pawn in the centre.
2. Develop your pieces, take out your knights and bishops. Usually it's better to develop knights before bishops.
3. Don't move the same piece twice in the Opening unless it's for a very good reason.
4. Protect and attack.
5. Castle as quickly as possible.

Developing: moving pieces from their starting position to a square where they have more space to move or where they have more control over the opponent's game.

Take note of the importance of the centre in the Opening.

The MAJOR PIECES
Heavy Soldiers:

Your major pieces should not enter the centre of the game at the beginning. The initial work is left to the minor pieces.

Light Soldiers - "**Minor Pieces**":= Pawns, Knights and Bishops.
Heavy Soldiers - "**Major Pieces**":= Queens and Rooks.

Unlike the "Light Soldiers" (Pawns, Knights, Bishops), the "Heavy Soldiers" (Queens and Rooks) should not be put in the centre straightaway. You must deploy the "Heavy Soldiers" once the "Light Soldiers" have been released. The "Heavy Soldiers" do excellent work from the back line.

Keep this simple thought in mind: **"minimum exposure, maximum power"**.

Now that you have learnt the five principles of the Opening, this will give you a good start in a chess game. Up until now we have not spoken of the major pieces, the queen and the rooks. The major pieces are very powerful and valuable pieces, a bit like having two tanks and a rocket launcher. These pieces can impose major damage on your opponent's pieces and territory. At the same time, you must be really careful with them. When using the major pieces it is important to have a clear plan, in order that you don't put them in danger.

1. Be Careful / Minimum Exposure
Your major pieces are important to your eventual victory, therefore you must be very careful with them. The queen and rooks should fire at the enemy from a distance at the rear of the field, where enemy units cannot easily attack them. It's a good idea to move your queen off the back rank, bring her into play and free up the back rank for the rooks to move along. Don't bring her out too far into the battlefield though, where she could be very exposed to attacks. Castling is a good way to hide and protect your king. Minimum exposure on the king is extremely important.

2. Be Powerful / Maximum Power
Castling is a good way to get your rooks out to play. Get them into the centre and working together. It would be really brilliant if you can move your rooks to an open or half-open file. Your idea should be to have both the rooks and the queen in strong positions but not too far forward. Clearing the way for your rooks and giving them lots of mobility is definitely a good strategy.

Open Files and Half-Open Files

Pawns need to be cleared out of the way to give the rooks space for action.
An "open file" has no pawns on it. A "half-open file" has pawns of one colour on it.

An **"open file"** is a file without pawns.
A **"half-open file"** is a file with only one pawn or pawns of only one colour.

Opening Principles

1. Open with a central pawn.
2. Develop pieces into the centre.
3. Develop with threats. Don't exchange without considered thought.
4. Develop as quickly as possible.
5. Don't take the queen out too early.
6. Make as few pawn moves as possible.
7. Develop your minor pieces early in the game. Develop knights before bishops.
8. Develop the knights on f3 and c3 if you are White or f6 and c6 if you are Black. Knights have much more power in the centre.
9. Keep the knights close to the centre if you can. "Knights on the rim are dim" - they may as well be picking flowers!
10. Don't move the same piece twice without very good reason.
11. If possible develop a different piece in each move.
12. Try not to block your bishops with pawns on the diagonals.
13. Castle as quickly as possible. Consider which side of the board you wish to castle.
14. Don't play for an early checkmate. **Attack after development.**
15. Clean out your back rank so that your rooks will have space to work together.
    Rooks work very well as a team.
16. Try to prevent your opponent from castling. Keep your opponent's king gripped in the centre if you can, easier said than done!
17. Don't move pawns in front of your castled king without good reason, these pawns are like foot soldiers protecting the king, and don't let a "hole" develop around your castled king.
18. **ALWAYS PLAY TO GAIN CONTROL OF THE CENTRE OF THE BOARD**.
19. Try to keep at least one pawn in the centre.
20. Don't sacrifice without good reason.

    For a sacrificed pawn you must
    - Gain extra moves, gain tempo (in order to initiate an attack) *or*
    - Deflect the enemy queen *or*
    - Prevent Castling *or*
    - Build up a strong attack.

Studying a Position

**When studying a position
it is important to consider the following points:**

1. **Enemy threats**
   – Be careful of those devilish attacks from your opponent!!
2. **Power of the pieces**
   – This is about your pieces and their mobility and strength on the chess board.
3. **Pawn structure**
   – Are your pawns looking after each other, protecting the king and defending territory?
4. **Piece mobility**
   – their freedom to move. Do your pieces have space to move around?
5. **King safety**
   – Is your king safe and in hiding?

11
TACTICS & STRATEGY

Time now to concentrate on the fun tactics and strategy!

Tactics are the backbone of chess.
Here are a few tactical tricks you should know:

the **PIN**
the **SKEWER**
the **FORK**,
DISCOVERED ATTACK,
DISCOVERED CHECK.

Tactics

the PIN
the SKEWER
the FORK
DISCOVERED ATTACK
DISCOVERED CHECK

Pin

In diagram 1. As you can see, the **black knight** on c6 cannot move. The movement of the knight would expose an attack on the king from the white bishop on b5, and it is illegal in chess to move into check. The knight is caught, it cannot move. It is said that the knight is **pinned**. At the same time, if black moves the **knight** on f6 White would be able to capture black's queen and Black would certainly not like to lose the queen. Therefore the black knight on f6 in also **pinned**.

Do you see a white piece that is pinned?

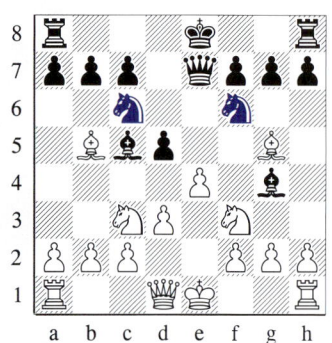

Diagram 1

Skewer

In diagram 2 the **black king** is in check. The **white queen** on h8 places the **king** in check. Black must immediately move the king out of check.

Remember the three ways to move out of check?

1. Move the king. 2. Capture the attacker. 3. Block the attack.

Black has no choice, the king must go to e7 and exposes an attack where the **white queen** can capture the **black queen**. This is called a **skewer**.

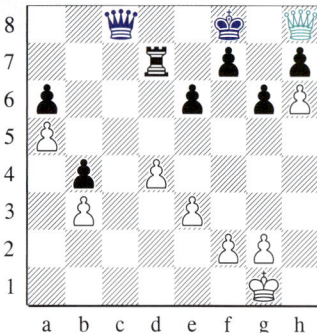

Diagram 2

Fork

Knight Fork

Diagram 3. The **black knight** is attacking the **white king** and the **white queen** at the same time. A double attack like this in chess is called a **fork**. White must move out of check immediately and therefore the queen is lost, a little tear for White! Boo Hoo!

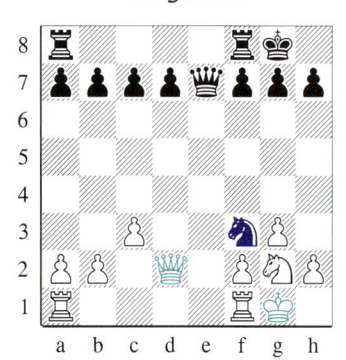

Diagram 3

...Tactics

Bishop Fork
In diagram 4 the **white bishop** captures the **pawn** on d5 (**Bxd5**) and is then forking the **rook** (on a8) and **knight** (on e6)
Remember how the rook is more powerful than the knight.
- *Rook: 5 points; Knight: 3 points.*

Black cannot save both pieces. Because of this Black must lose one of them. Do you see any move where Black can escape from this dreadful situation or even make it less painful?

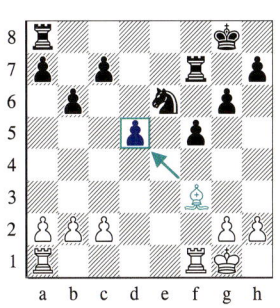

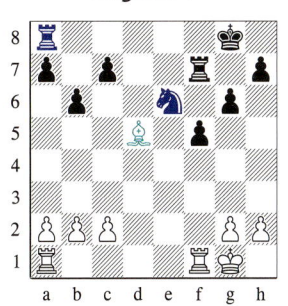

Answer:....................

Why?:......................................

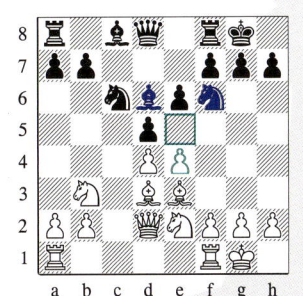

Diagram 4

Pawn Fork
It is White's move in diagram 5 on the left. White decides to move the **pawn** on e4 forward to **e5** instead of capturing the d-pawn. This is a good decision. After this move Black has a few considerations. Black is under a dangerous double attack from the pawn, a **fork**.

Diagram 5

Black must do something to minimise the damage.

1. Run with the **bishop** to b8 or c7; then ex**f6** and gxf6 and Black loses the knight to a pawn and a big hole in the castling position. This is extremely bad!
2. Take the e-pawn with the **bishop** (**Bxe5**); dxe5 and Nxe5. Two pawns for one bishop. Getting a little better but this is still not very good!
3. Can you see how White can escape from this fork unscathed?
   If Black can attack White somewhere with one of the forked pieces, the **knight** or the **bishop**, perhaps Black can rescue the position.
   Do you see it?..

Answers:
Pin: The white pawn on e4 which cannot capture diagonally. The white knight on f3 is also pinned.
Bishop Fork: R-e8, the rook escapes and protects the knight on e6 at the same time. If White decides to capture the knight, Black can now recapture with both sides still level on material.
Pawn Fork: B-b4, attacking the white queen. The white queen must first escape from this attack and Black has time to run with the knight. PHEW! BRILL!! Everything safe, but that was a little uncomfortable for a while! Watch the forks!

...Tactics

Discovered Check (& Discovered Attack)

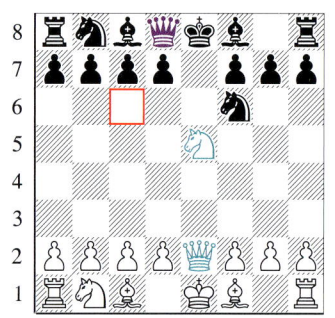

Diagram 6:
If the **white knight** in the centre (e5) moves, the black king will be in check from the **white queen**. This is a **Discovered Check**
With this power, the knight can move to the square **c6**, attacking the **black queen** with the **knight** and revealing the check attack from the **white queen** at the same time. The king must directly move out of check. Black cannot escape from check and save the **queen**. There is not much choice here. The **black queen** is lost. The name of the check following the knight move is called a **Discovered Check**

Diagram 6

> A **discovered check** occurs when a player moves a piece that reveals a hidden piece that attacks the enemy king.

> A **discovered attack** occurs when a player moves a piece that reveals a hidden piece that attacks an enemy piece.

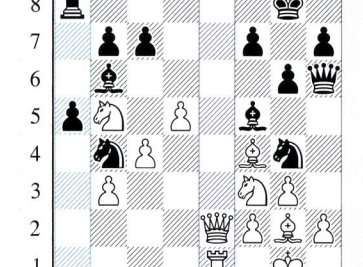

Open File and Half-Open File

There are no pawns on an "open file".
There are only pawns of one colour on a "half-open file".

Pawns must be cleared out of the way for rooks to manoeuvre.
Diagram 7:
a-File: This is a **half-open file** as there is only one black pawn on it. This is a good file to place rooks and queens where they have lots of mobility.
e-File: This is an **open file** as there are no pawns on it. This is a great file for the white rook and white queen to work together as seen in the diagram.

Diagram 7

> **There are no pawns on an open file.**
> **There are only pawns of one colour on a half-open file.**

...Tactics

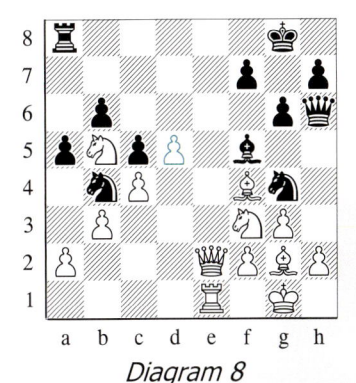

Diagram 8

The Passed Pawn

In chess, the **passed pawn** is an unblocked pawn. A passed pawn has no opposite-coloured pawn ahead on either file beside it or on the same file in front of it to hinder its journey to the eighth rank.

In diagram 8, the **passed pawn** is the white pawn on **d5**. These pawns are very strong and a great advantage to have. In order to prevent the advance of the **passed pawn** the opposition must use a powerful piece to block it, thereby sacrificing its powers.

There is more information on the **passed pawn** in Chapter 12 "The Passed Pawn", page 93.

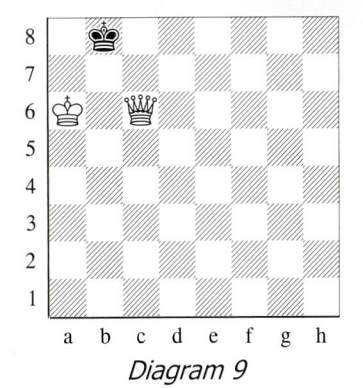

Diagram 9

The Queen with too much Power!

If all you have left is a king, don't forget that you can still get a draw with stalemate ("Games Ending in a Draw", page 67). In diagram 9, White has an extra powerful queen, but unfortunately for White the queen has too much power and the player has fallen into stalemate. The king can never move into check and currently the king is not in check. Black has no legal move and the game is a draw. This happens quite often with chess players that are learning the game, and also to experienced chess players in competitions when under time pressure from the chess clock. In other words - be careful! Especially be careful with queens in the endgame. Don't try to get lots of queens to deliver checkmate. All you need is one queen against a lone king. Keep it simple!

Pawns & Tactics

Isolated Pawn:
weak / strong

An **isolated pawn** is a pawn without a pawn of the same colour on either file beside it. In the endgame, the isolated pawn can be quite weak as it has no other pawns protecting it. Remember how pawns are excellent at looking after each other?

Doubled Pawns:
weak

When there are two pawns of the same colour on the same file, these are **doubled pawns.** This occurs when a pawn captures a piece diagonally to a file where another pawn already exists.

Triple Pawns:
weak

Three pawns of the same colour on a single file.

Backward Pawn:
weak

A **backward pawn** is a pawn which has no other pawns of the same colour looking after it from behind. A backward pawn gets no support from another pawn and is usually quite weak.

Passed Pawn:
strong

In chess, a **passed pawn** is a pawn without obstruction; a pawn without a pawn of the opposite colour directly or diagonally in front of it, obstructing its journey to the final rank.

Protected Passed Pawn:
Very strong

A **protected passed pawn** is a passed pawn that is protected by another pawn.

Hanging Pawn:
weak / strong

Hanging pawns occur when pawns of the same colour exist beside each other without support from neighbouring pawns on either side. Sometimes these pawns are advantageous but very often these are weak pawns as there are no pawns protecting them. It depends on the position.

Promoted Pawn:
very strong

This is a pawn that is promoted to the eight rank where it can be exchanged for a queen, rook, knight or bishop.

Gambit Pawn:
Be careful!

A **gambit pawn** is a pawn that is offered as a sacrifice in order to get an advantage (a space advantage, a tempo advantage or a strategy advantage) in the Opening.

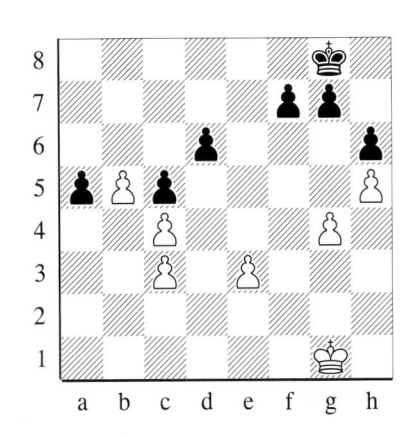

ISOLATED PAWN: e3 (White)

DOUBLED PAWNS: c3 & c4 (White)

TRIPLE PAWNS: There aren't any

BACKWARD PAWN: g4 (White), d6 (Black)

PASSED PAWN: a5 (Black) & b5 (White)

Lesson 10

THE PAWN

Look at the diagram below and pick out examples of the following pawns:

ISOLATED PAWN?
[ ] White / Black

DOUBLED PAWNS?
[ ] White / Black

TRIPLE PAWNS?
[ ] White / Black

BACKWARD PAWN?
[ ] White / Black

PASSED PAWN?
[ ] White / Black

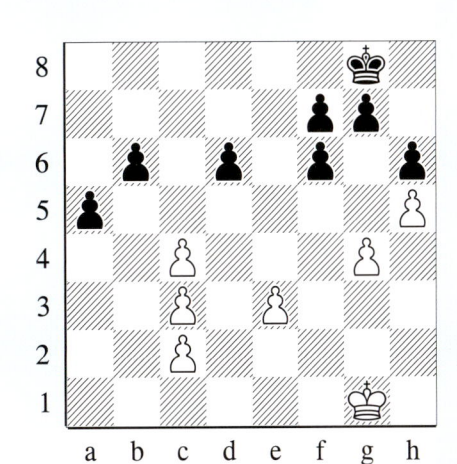

Pawn Structure

How do you make it safe?

1. Try to keep at least one pawn in the centre.
2. Pawns are good when working together.
3. If possible don't move a pawn in front of your protected castled king.
    These pawns work brilliantly as a defence for your king.
4. Don't constrain your bishops with pawns.
    Develop bishops before blocking diagonals.
5. Make as few pawn moves as possible.
6. Don't sacrifice a pawn without good reason.

   For a sacrificed pawn you must

   - Gain extra moves (ie. gain tempo in order to initiate an attack) *or*
   - Deflect the enemy queen *or*
   - Prevent castling *or*
   - Build up a strong attack.

***Pawn Structure*:**
Your pawn structure is the manner in which your pawns are laid out on the board.
Pawns work best when they are placed diagonally protecting each other.
The pawn in the smallest piece and the piece with the least mobility. It is the only piece that cannot move backwards. Pawns are nonetheless very important pieces.

Lesson 11

Tactics

SOME TACTICAL PUZZLES

Study the following diagrams. Do you see the tactic to use in one move to win material?

Write in the tactical move:
1. **Fork** / 2. **Skewer** / 3. **Pin** / 4. **Discovered Check**

White's move in each case

Write in the **move**, the name of the **tactic** employed, the **piece** or **pieces won**, and the **points won** ("Value of the Pieces", page 29), (this is the difference between the points gained and the points lost).

Move:	Tactic name:
Piece won:	Points won:

⇧ 1

Move:	Tactic name:
Piece won:	Points won:

⇧ 2

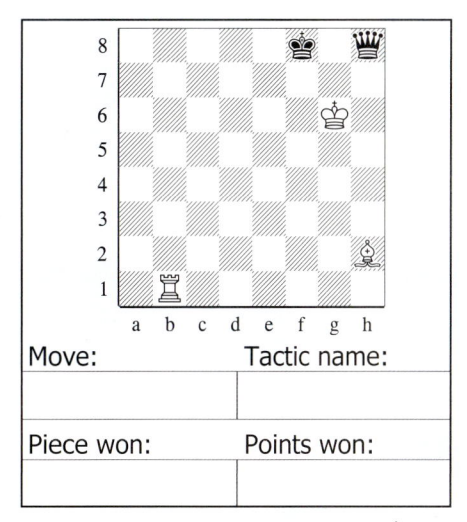

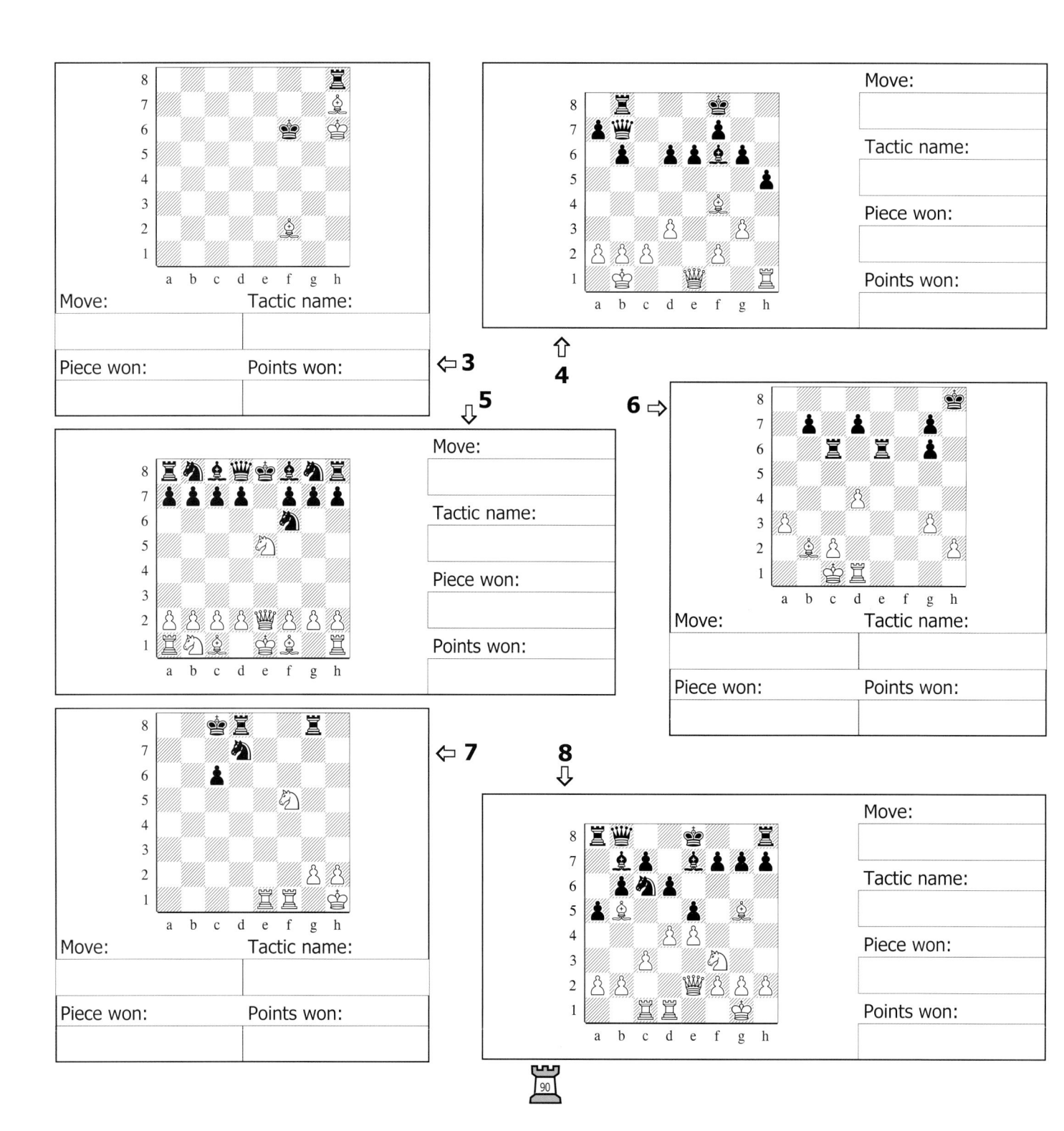

3 ⇐

Move:

Tactic name:

Piece won:

Points won:

4 ⇑

Move:

Tactic name:

Piece won:

Points won:

5 ⇓

Move:

Tactic name:

Piece won:

Points won:

6 ⇒

Move:

Tactic name:

Piece won:

Points won:

7 ⇐

Move:

Tactic name:

Piece won:

Points won:

8 ⇓

Move:

Tactic name:

Piece won:

Points won:

Middlegame Principles

Tactics are the heart of the middlegame when the two armies are out fighting. Here are a few tips that are important to consider in order to get a better position in the middlegame:

1. Avoid serious pawn weaknesses.
2. In cramped positions free yourself with exchanges.
3. Don't bring your king out while your opponent's queen in still in play.
4. Know **when** and **where** you should **exchange** pieces.

    When you are up material try to exchange, especially queens.

    Exchange pawns when you are down major or minor pieces.

5. When you are material ahead, exchange pieces, especially queens. Pieces are exchanged when you capture an enemy piece and they capture your piece back. It is always good to exchange queens when you are material ahead.
6. If your opponent has one or more pieces exposed, look for a combination.

    A combination is a sequence of moves that lead to an advantage in your position.

7. There must be something in the position that suggests a plan.

    A plan must be flexible and short. A plan must be based on the following principles:

    - Enemy threats.
    - Material.
    - Pawn structure.
    - Piece mobility.
    - King safety.

8. In superior positions, to attack the enemy king you must open a file (or diagonal) for your major pieces (rooks and queens).
9. In inferior positions, the best defence is to counter-attack, if possible.
10. There should be a plan in every position.
11. Develop queens and rooks on open files and bishops on open diagonals.
12. Develop pieces working together on open diagonals or files.
13. Be careful of isolated pawns.
14. Play with the pieces, not pawns.

Middlegame Principles

15. Don't ignore your opponent's move. Examine every threat.
16. Rely on your own good judgement and don't ever think that your opponent does not see your tactical manoeuvres or ideas.
17. Attack your opponent with pieces, not just with one single piece.
18. If you are ahead in development, attack!
19. If you are behind in development, keep the position closed.
20. Mobility and activity of your pieces are very important.
21. Two bishops can be a real advantage.
22. Keep a watchful eye on passed pawns. They say that the passed pawn is the heart of the endgame.
23. Often one extra pawn is not enough to win.
24. Keep an eye on doubled pawns, isolated pawns and blocked pawns. This is true for the endgame as well as the middlegame.
25. Know when a knight is stronger than a bishop, and vice versa.
26. Move pawns to open files or diagonals or to open up space for pieces. Pawn moves can change the position or state of the game greatly so give considered thought to every pawn move.
27. Develop rooks on open files, half-open files or on a file that will soon be open.
28. Watch the mobility of your bishops when you are fixing your pawns.
29. Attack pinned pieces.
30. Attack weak opponent pawns.
31. Keep your pawn structure safe and try to destroy your opponent's pawn structure.
32. Be careful with pawn moves. Be certain that you have good reason with every pawn move. Move pawns to make space for your pieces and to attack the centre.
33. Capture in the direction of the centre with pawns. When you have a choice with pawns, capture towards the centre.
34. In even positions, centralise the action of all your pieces.

12
THE PASSED PAWN

We must now deal with the passed pawn before approaching the endgame.

The Passed Pawn

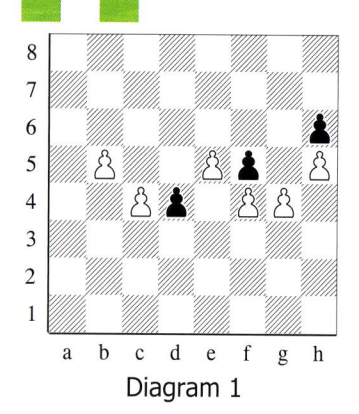

In chess, a **passed pawn** is**:**

A pawn without restraint from an opposite coloured pawn. The **passed pawn** is an unblocked pawn, a pawn that has no opposite coloured pawn directly or diagonally in front of it and is on its way to promotion without hindrance from an enemy pawn.

In the diagram on the left the white passed pawns are **b5**, **c4**, and **e5**. The black pawn on **d4** is also a passed pawn. If black plays fxg4, then Black would have an extra passed pawn on **g4**. These passed pawns are an added advantage as your opponent would have to use a powerful piece to block the journey of the pawn or perhaps even exchange a powerful piece for the pawn, not a sacrifice you would like to consider if at all possible.

Diagram 1

White passed pawns:
b5, **c4**, and **e5**.
Black passed pawn:
d4.

In chess, a **passed** pawn is a pawn that has no enemy pawns blocking its way to promotion. The passed pawn is without any enemy pawn on the same file in front or on either file beside it in front of it on its journey forward. This pawn is a very powerful pawn on its **journey to promotion or queening**.
If you have a passed pawn, run with it!

The Outside Passed Pawn

An outside passed pawn is a passed pawn that is placed on files **a** or **h** and is separated by at least one file from the other pawns. For example, an **a**-pawn in diagram 2 on the right is an outside passed pawn.

Very often this is an advantage. In this instance the outside passed pawn on **a4** is very strong. The black king must block the queening journey of the a-pawn by moving away from the centre of the board. White is then free to travel in the direction of the black pawns with the intention of gobbling them up and promoting one of its own kingside pawns.

White wins with 1. a5, g5 2. a6, h5 3. a7, K-b7 4. K-d5, e4 5. fxe4, fxe4 6. Kxe4, and the white king chews up the remaining black pawns leaving White's kingside pawns free to travel up the board and promote.

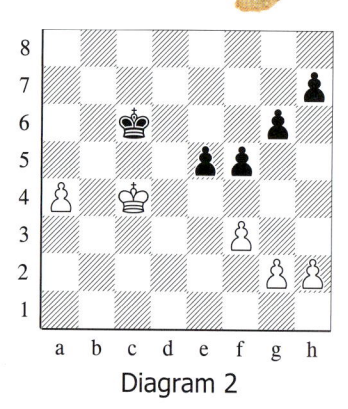

Diagram 2

The material is level but White wins as it has a distinct advantage having an outside passed pawn on **a4**.

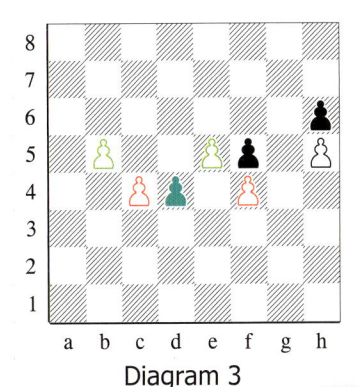

Protected Passed Pawn

A protected passed pawn is a passed pawn that is protected by another pawn.

Diagram 3 - **Protected Passed Pawns**:
These are the white passed pawns on files **b** and **e** which are protected by friendly pawns **c** and **f.**

Diagram 3

White's passed pawns: **b5**, **c4**, and **e5**.
White's protected passed pawns: **b5** and **e5**.
Black's passed pawn: **d4**.
The pawns on files-**c** and **f** are importantly defending White's passed pawns on **b5** and **e5**.

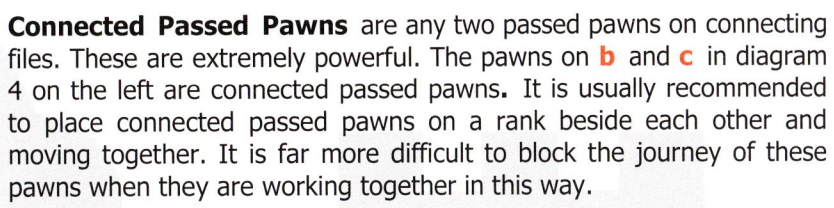

Connected Passed Pawns

Connected Passed Pawns are any two passed pawns on connecting files. These are extremely powerful. The pawns on **b** and **c** in diagram 4 on the left are connected passed pawns**.** It is usually recommended to place connected passed pawns on a rank beside each other and moving together. It is far more difficult to block the journey of these pawns when they are working together in this way.

Look at diagram 4 on the left. This is a really interesting position illustrating the power of connected passed pawns. Black has a bishop and a queen while White only has two pawns. Black to play.

White is hoping to play b7#
Black's choices:
if 1...Q-g8; 2. b7#
if 1...Q-d8; 2. cxd8(Q)+, B-b8; b7#;
if 1...Q-d5; 2. c8(Q)+, B-b8; 3. b7+, Qxb7+; 4. Qxb7#;
if 1...Q-g6; 2. c8(Q)+, B-b8; 3. Q-b7#;
if 1...Q-a5+; 2. Kxa5, K-b7; 3. bxa7 and black's king can only stop one of the two white pawns from promoting
if 1...Q-a5+; 2. Kxa5, Bxb6+; 3. Kxb6 and black's remaining piece, the king has no legal move and is in "Stalemate". The game is drawn.

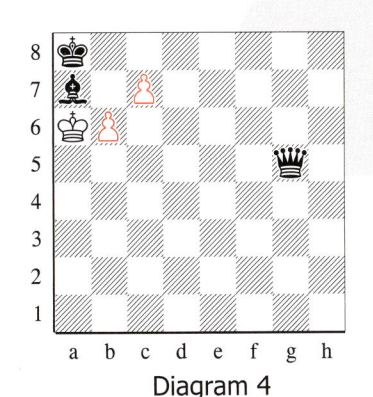

Diagram 4

Position after **c7!!**
White has two connected passed pawns that restrain Black's army of queen and bishop.

The Passed Pawn:

Creating a Passed Pawn

The **Passed Pawn** is the pawn most likely to journey to the eighth rank where it can transpose to another more powerful piece. Passed pawns are essential as part of the endgame. Whenever you can, try to create passed pawns and look after them well. Watch out for threats of your opponent creating a passed pawn.

A passed pawn must move quickly but safely. Block your opponent's passed pawns as effectively as possible without losing power from your own pieces.

Keep a Sharp Eye on Passed Pawns

Passed pawns are very very dangerous. Because of this it is really really important to keep a sharp eye on these naughty creatures.

Block your Opponent's Passed Pawn with a King or Knight

It often happens that you must block your opponent's passed pawn with your own piece in front of it. The best piece to do this is your **king, knight** or **bishop**. As well as blocking the passed pawn, you must consider that your piece will now lose a lot of power. By blocking the pawn, your piece is therefore rendered somewhat immobile - not so good for a powerful piece. The major pieces don't work so well in blocking pawns. They are far too powerful to be put on such a menial task.

A Rook sits very comfortably behind a Passed Pawn

This works irrespective of whether the passed pawn belongs to you or your opponent.

If you have a Passed Pawn, RUN RUN RUN with it!
Carefully, mind you!

Lesson 12

Promoting the Passed Pawn: Queening

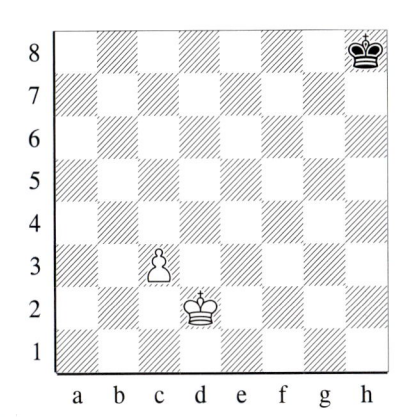

White would like to promote the **c3** pawn to **c8** to create a **queen**. With a queen working alongside the king it is not too difficult to get checkmate.

If Black can place the **king** in front of the **pawn** and block its path, Black can get a draw. Can White stop this? If White can destroy Black's plans, White can win.

Let's have a look.

White to move.
Play this game with a friend and see if you can position the black king in front of the c-pawn and thereby stopping the journey of promoting the pawn.

If you don't work it out in the first go change sides and try again with the pieces back to the position in the diagram.

Lesson 13

The Passed Pawn In the Endgame

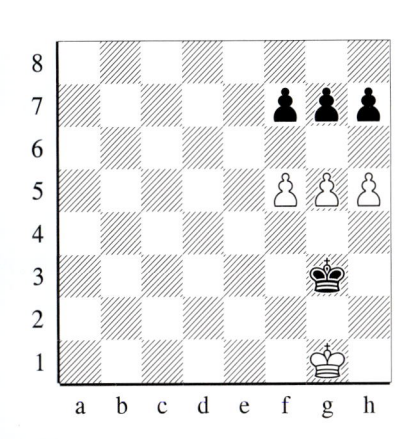

Play this game with a friend.

White to start.
Who can manage to get a passed pawn first and promote to a queen?

Now explore with Black to start. Who can manage to promote a pawn?

13
THE GREEK GIFT
A serious tactical trick, you could have a lot of fun with this...

The Greek Gift

Origin of The "Greek Gift"
The Trojan War was a very famous mythical battle between the Trojans and the Achaeans (Greeks). The battle continued for ten years and the sides were so evenly matched that it seemed that the war might never end. The war is one of the most important events in Greek mythology. One thing the Greeks had that the Trojans lacked was the cunning mind of Odysseus. Odysseus was one of the first Greek mythical heroes renowned for his brain as well as his muscle. He devised the idea of a Trojan Horse. The Greeks pretended to retreat and the Trojans pulled the horse into their city as a victory trophy. When the Trojan Horse was left at the gates of Troy, the Trojans took their "trophy" within their walls, little knowing that the belly of the beast was filled with armed soldiers who would soon destroy their city.

The Trojan Horse
The Trojan War ended with a gift, a trick! - A Wooden Horse called the Trojan Horse.

"Beware of the Greeks bearing gifts!"
Have you ever heard this phrase? It's good to take heed sometimes, especially when playing chess!

Let's learn the "Greek Gift" sacrifice in Chess
'The Greek Gift' sacrifice is a theme in chess that you simply cannot afford to ignore. This involves the sacrifice of bishop at h7 (or h2 for Black) and is followed by a N-g5+ or combinations of attack generated by queen and knight. Even when the sacrifice is not perfectly sound it is tricky to refute. It can be pretty brutal. Also be aware that there is only a hairline difference in positions or patterns where these types of attacks may succeed or fail.

The "Greek Gift" Sacrifice
Here is the "Greek Gift" in action:

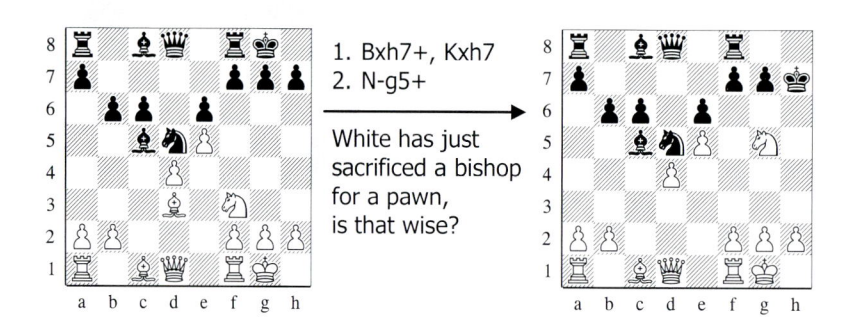

1. Bxh7+, Kxh7
2. N-g5+

White has just sacrificed a bishop for a pawn, is that wise?

...The Greek Gift

The "Greek Gift" Sacrifice

Response and follow through to the "Greek Gift":

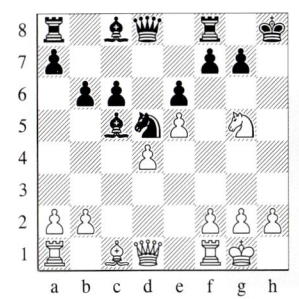

A. What would you do if Black played K-h8?

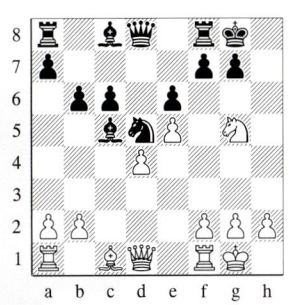

B. What would you do if Black played K-g8?

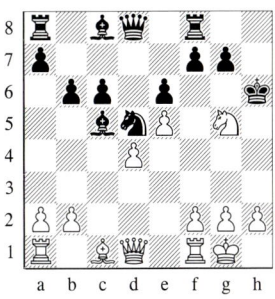

C. What would you do if Black played K-h6?

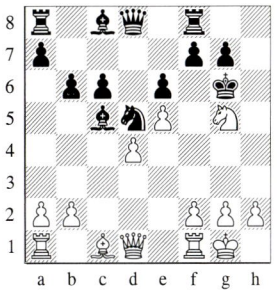

D. What would you do if Black played K-g6?

Answers to the Greek Gift:
A. K-h8; Q-h5+, K-g8; Q-h7#.
B. K-g8; Q-h5, R-e8; Qxf7+, K-h8; Q-h5+, K-g8; Q-h7+, K-f8; Q-h8+, K-e7; Qxg7#.
C. K-h6; Nxe6, and the Black Queen is now lost. K-h7; Q-h5+, K-g8; Nxd8 or K-g6; Nxd8.
D. K-g6; Now that's a whole different ball game. The queen is usually best coming to g4 but you'll just have to analyse each position and see how you can get all your forces to work together for a brutal attack while the black king is looking a little exposed out from under the cover of his foot soldiers.

102

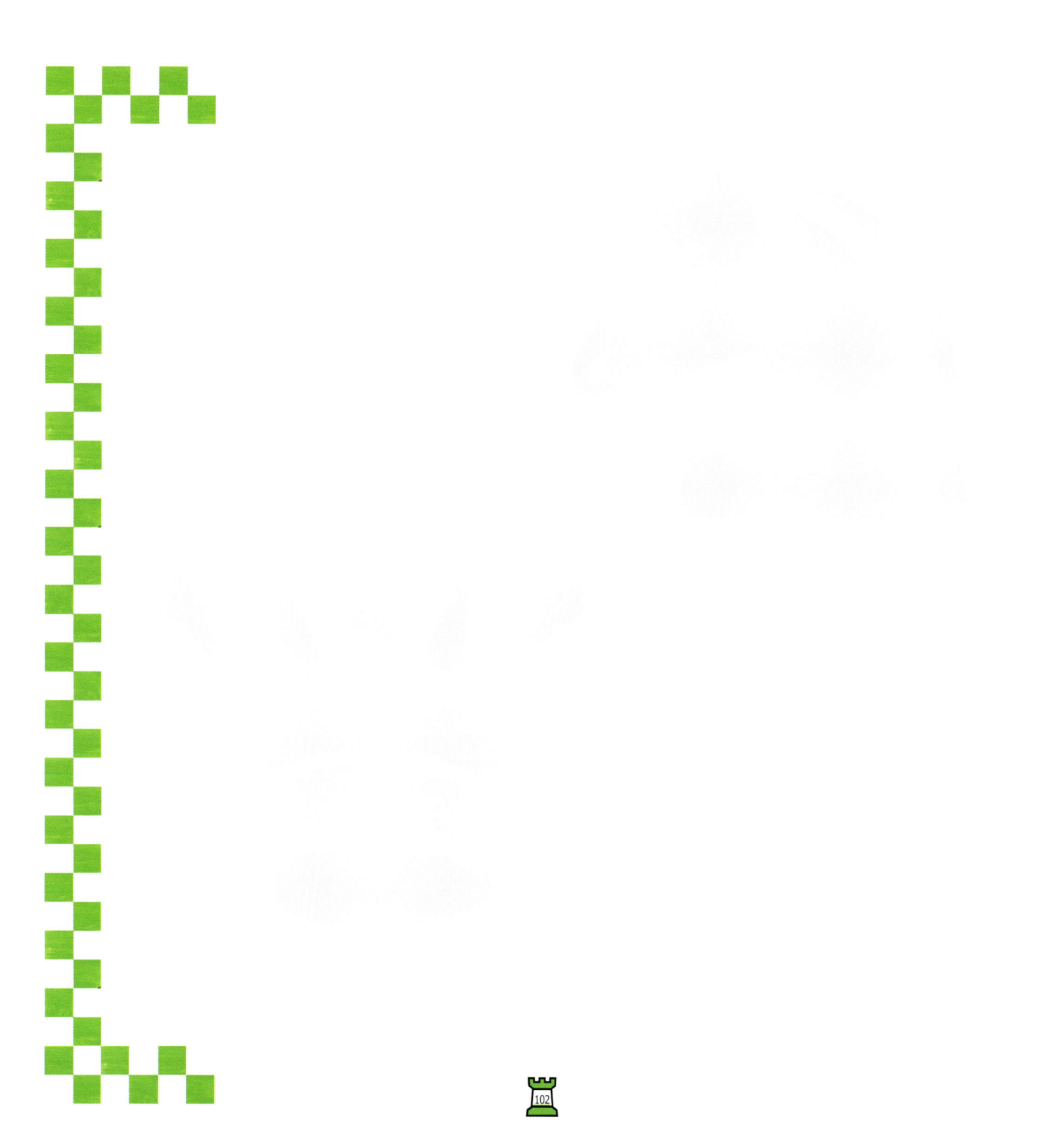

14
THE ENDGAME

Believe it or not, this can be the most difficult part of the game. Take note of the ideas and recommendations in this section.

End Game Principles

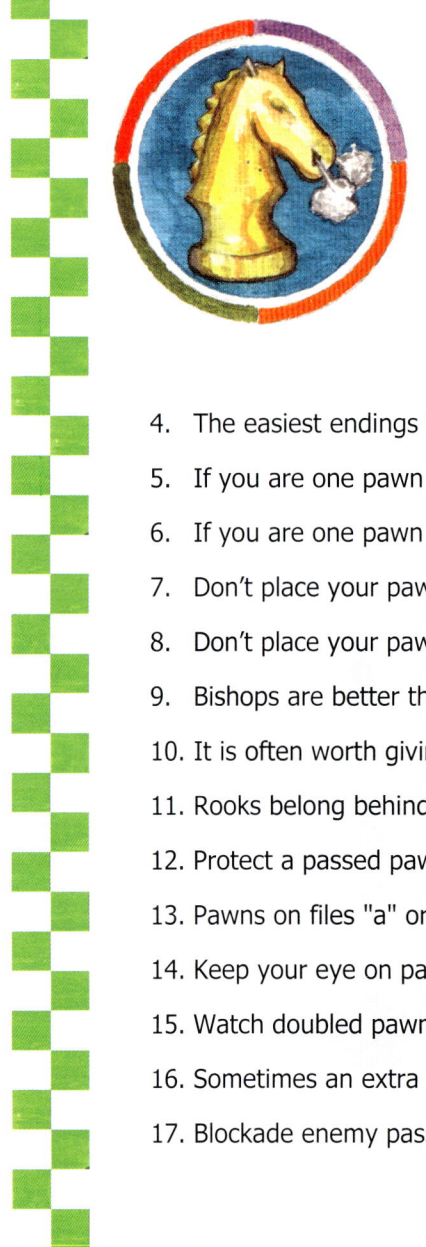

1. To win without pawns, you must be at least a rook or two minor pieces ahead. ("Check & Checkmate", page 39).
2. Passed pawns must be pushed. ("The Passed Pawn", page 93).
3. The king must be active in the ending. Activate your king once the enemy queen is off the board.
4. The easiest endings to win are pure pawn endings. (i.e. only pawns and kings left in the game).
5. If you are one pawn ahead, exchange pieces (queens, rooks, knights, bishops), not pawns.
6. If you are one pawn down, exchange pawns, not pieces.
7. Don't place your pawns on the same colour squares as your bishop.
8. Don't place your pawns on the same colour squares as your opponent's bishop.
9. Bishops are better than knights in all but blocked pawn positions in the endgame.
10. It is often worth giving up a pawn to get a rook on the seventh rank.
11. Rooks belong behind passed pawns. Keep your rook behind a passed pawn, not in front.
12. Protect a passed pawn with a king in front of it or a rook behind it.
13. Pawns on files "a" or "h" are difficult to promote and these games often end in a draw.
14. Keep your eye on passed pawns. The passed pawn is one of the most powerful pieces in the endgame.
15. Watch doubled pawns and isolated pawns. This is true for the endgame as well as the middlegame.
16. Sometimes an extra pawn is not enough to win, particularly in rook and pawn endings.
17. Blockade enemy passed pawns with your king or a minor piece.

15
CHESS PLAYERS ON DIFFERENT LEVELS

Here's a bit of fun if you are playing someone that is much weaker or stronger than you.

Chess Players on Different Levels

If there are chess players on different levels, try to start the game with these positions.
The stronger player being White and White to play in each game.

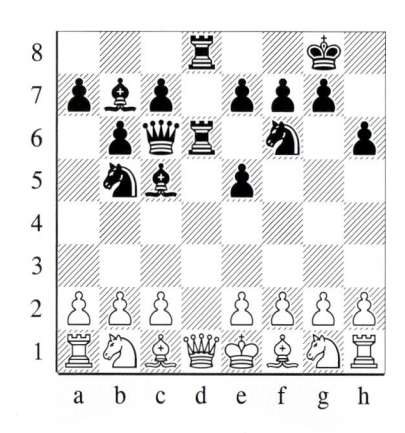

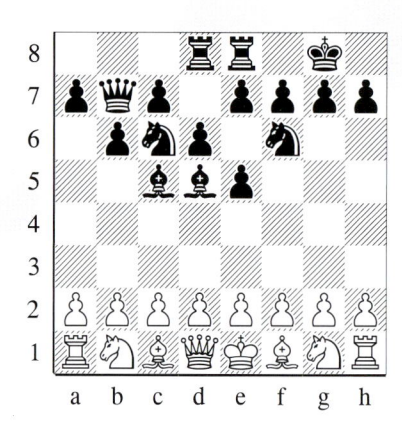

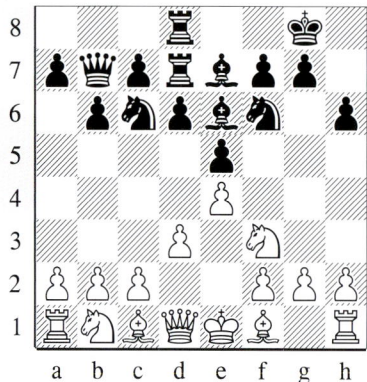

16
A GAME FROM BOBBY FISCHER

This will take a little time but it's well worth it.
Take out your chess board and pieces to follow the game.

Bobby Fischer v Reuben Fine
New York, 1963

Robert James "Bobby" Fischer (March 9th, 1943 – January 17, 2008)

Bobby Fischer was born in America. He was famous as a very talented chess player as a teenager. Bobby Fischer was the first and only World Chess Champion from America. Fischer defeated Boris Spassky from the Soviet Union in Reykjavík, Iceland, in 1972.

Fischer is probably the most famous of all chess players and some say he was the most brilliant chess player ever. He died in Reykjavík in 2008. He was a very strange but brilliant man.

Here is a short game he played when he was very young. It's a good idea to go through the game slowly and imagine what was in the mind of Fischer while playing.

White: Bobby Fischer
Black: Reuben Fine

Position after Fischer plays 4. b4

Position after Fischer plays 8. Q-b3

	White	Black
1	e4	e5
2	N-f3	N-c6
3	B-c4	B-c5
4	b4	Bxb4
5	c3	B-a5
6	d4	exd4
7	0-0	dxc3
8	Q-b3	Q-e7
9	Nxc3	N-f6
10	N-d5	Nxd5
11	exd5	N-e5
12	Nxe5	Qxe5
13	B-b2	Q-g5
14	h4	Qxh4
15	Bxg7	R-g8
16	Rf-e1+	K-d8
17	Q-g3	1-0

...Bobby Fischer v Reuben Fine

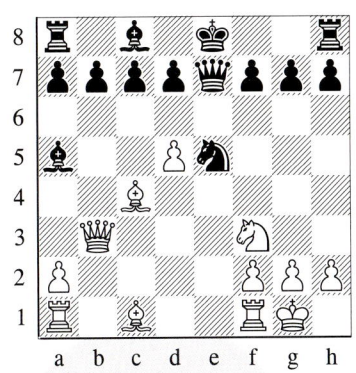

Position after Fine plays
11. ... N-e5

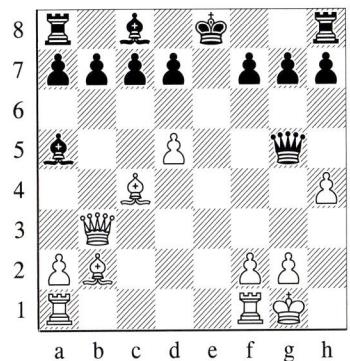

Position after Fischer plays
14. h4

This is the position at the end of the game when Fischer played Q-g3.

Do you know why Reuben Fine resigned?

Answer:
If ...Qxg3 then B-f6# (checkmate!)
If ...Rxg7 then Qxh4 (losing the queen)
If ...Q-e7; Rxe7, Kxe7; Q-e5+, K-d8; B-f6# (checkmate!)
Everything is dreadful! And lost!

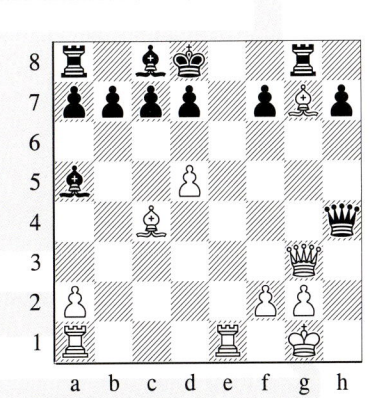

Section 4

A Real Game   113
More Puzzles   127
Puzzles & Lessons - Answers   135
Chess Puzzle from New Zealand 141

112

17
A REAL GAME

This will take some time so take out your chess board and pieces.

Analysis of a Real Game

Mark Quinn V Roman Chytilek
(Ireland)   (Czech Republic)

European Union Championships Under 20, Siofok, Hungary, 1996. Reti Opening

White	= Mark plays the white pieces
Black	= Roman plays the black pieces
white	= white piece
black	= black piece
1.xxx	= white's move
1… xxx	= black's move

We are now ready to look at a serious game.
In order to go through this game it is important to have a chess board and pieces in front of you. Go through the game nice and slowly and take note of the ideas in every move.

1. N-f3

Although many players open with a pawn in the centre it is also possible to delay this but always keep in mind the idea of eventually taking control of the centre with support from pawns. If you play what is often called a "quiet" move, in other words not challenging anything immediately, be sure not to let your opponent take full control of the centre. In the first couple of moves, d4 or d5 (more than any other moves) give you lots of space in the opening, which can lead to a big advantage if your opponent is slow to react and stake a claim to the centre themselves. With e4 the queen and the bishop are ready to come out - as well as knights, and there is a pawn putting pressure on the centre. Be prepared to play the pawn into the centre when you're ready. Nonetheless f3 is a natural and strong square for the knight. The knight is developed toward the centre and ready to take part in any future battles there. Whatever happens in the centre of the board affects the rest of the board.

Now what does Roman have in mind?!

1. …   b6

Roman also plays a "quiet" move. This simple pawn move leaves a nice opening for Roman's white squared bishop. From b7 the bishop will exert pressure on the long diagonal right across the board. Movement of pawns must be clearly thought out. Make as few pawn moves as possible in the opening. Pawns don't move backwards so you should have a clear idea in mind when you move them. Pawns also have extra strength when they support each other.

Lesson 1:
Don't forget the strategic plan in the opening:
__Make as few pawn moves as possible in the opening. Focus on developing your pieces.__

Lesson 2:
__Don't move pawns without good reason.__

2. g3
Mark challenges Roman's attempt to control the long diagonal (h1-a8) by preparing to place his white squared bishop on g2.

2. ...   B-b7
Roman develops his first piece by placing the bishop on the long diagonal, dominating the squares b7-e4 across the board. This enables him to keep tabs on Mark's white squared g2 bishop when it comes out. This is an ideal development move for Roman's white squared bishop. He has followed through on his plan which started with 1. ... b6.

Lesson 3:
__If you play a move with a specific idea or plan be sure to follow through with your plan immediately before initiating a new plan or course of action.__

3. B-g2 (Diagram 1)
This is a sensible and logical development move which attempts to neutralise Roman's fianchetto bishop. Mark is now ready to castle. Take a moment to see how useful 3. B-g2 is:
1.   It develops a minor piece.
2.   It puts extra pressure on the centre.
3.   It prepares for castling.

Lesson 4:
__In the opening, try to have at least two ideas or reasons for every move.__

Lesson 5:
Don't forget the key strategic plan in the opening:
__Keep pressure on the centre__

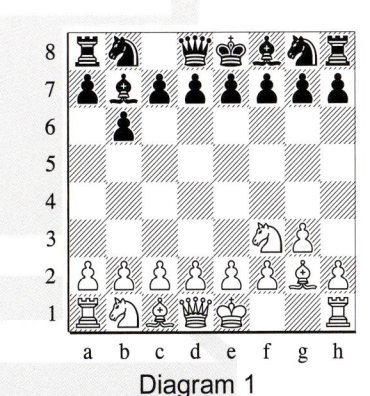

Diagram 1

Lesson 6:
Another key Opening Principle is:
> **Develop as early as possible by moving out your <u>minor pieces</u> early,**
> **Be careful with your queen:**
> **don't take her out too early, she might be chased or worse still captured.**

3. ...   g6

Roman prepares to develop his other bishop on the long diagonal. Note that Roman has still not developed the knights. Roman has to be careful here as Mark can now seize the centre.

Lesson 7:
> **Place your pieces in a position where they have the most power and mobility.**
> **This is usually in the centre.**
> **Sometimes however, a bishop on the long diagonal can be very powerful in a corner and exert pressure across the whole board.**

4. d4

Mark develops a central pawn and takes control of the centre. Mark's black squared bishop can now develop to active squares like f4 & g5 depending on where Roman develops his pieces.

4. ...   B-g7

Roman completes his plan, fianchettoing both his bishops. He is still a long way from castling because he has not moved either of his knights. Mark, on the other hand, is ready to castle.

Lesson 8:
> **Castle as quickly as possible.**

5. 0-0 (Diagram 2)

Clever move! Mark's king is now safe, protected behind his kingside pawns. He's a smart chess player! He has a perfect fianchettoed castled position. Mark could also have castled on the queenside but this would have taken more time. Mark wants to get his king's rook into the game as soon as possible.

Great chess players would always advise you to move your kingside pieces out first as you only have to move two pieces out in order to be ready for castling. On the queenside you must move three pieces out before you are prepared for castling. It is important to castle as early as possible.

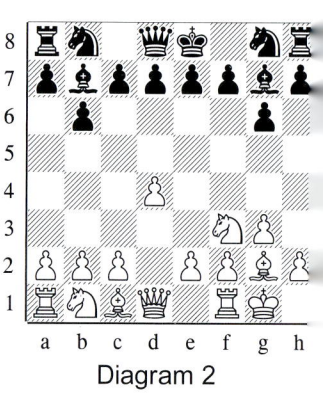

Diagram 2

5. ...   e6

Roman prepares an open path for the queen and knight while also exerting some pressure on the centre. He must be careful and prevent Mark from playing 6. e4, whereupon Mark would have complete control of the centre. Mark cannot play e4 yet as the bishop on b7 would capture the pawn. Once Mark plays N-c3, e4 may be possible. Roman needs to prevent this at all costs or Mark's pawns will chase Roman's knights away from the centre.

6. c4

The move c4 has many purposes:
- It attacks the d5 square.
- It also prepares future play on the c-file (once Mark has developed his bishop he will develop his rook to c1).
- Mark's queen can now go to b3 or a4 and exert pressure on Roman's queenside.
- The c-file is now ready to be utilised by the heavy pieces.
- If Roman wishes to play d5, c4xd5 would leave Roman with one less pawn in the centre.

Mark will try to exploit Roman's incomplete development. Mark has created lots of space for his pieces to start an attack on the queenside.

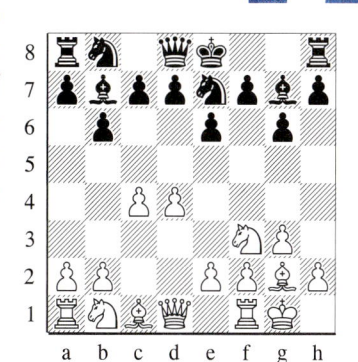

Diagram 3

6. ...   N-e7 (Diagram 3)

At last, Roman develops a knight. From e7 the black knight is coming into the centre to exert pressure in the centre and especially on the key d5 square (and also to give protection to the d-pawn). Generally it is a good idea to develop knights before bishops. The question is, will Mark be able to punish Roman's lack of development?

Lesson 9:
In general it is best to develop knights before bishops but sometimes it depends on the opening plan of your opponent. Your bishops may be best placed in the centre as opposed to the long diagonal. Developing knights before bishops allows you to configure best options for your bishops.

Roman is already under pressure and needs to castle quickly.

7. N-c3

A simple developing move and a natural square for the queenside knight. Mark now threatens to play 8. e4 with complete control of the centre.

Lesson 10:
Place your pieces in a position where they have the most power and mobility, usually in the centre.

> Take note of where the knights are placed.
> Sometimes learners put the knights on the side of the board but they are not as powerful there as they are in the centre. Remember the phrase: "knights on the rim are dim!"? Consider *diagram 4*. Look at how many squares both the black and white knights are attacking. Now look at *diagram 5*, when the knights are on the rim of the board. The knights have much fewer options from the side.

7. ...   d5

At last Roman challenges the centre and threatens to take the pawn on c4. If Mark chooses to exchange pieces with 8. cxd, Nxd5; 9. Nxd5, Bxd5, Roman is left with a very powerful piece in the centre of the board. To dislodge this powerful piece would be very difficult.

8. B-f4

Mark responds by quietly developing his bishop to f4 completing his development of minor pieces. If Roman decides to capture with dxc4 the white queen can check on a4 and recapture the pawn on c4 simultaneously placing the powerful queen in a dangerous position for Roman.

8. ...   0-0 (Diagram 6)

Roman sees Mark's devious plan and decides to avoid any dangers by castling.

Lesson 11:

Watch all checks.
Eliminate possible checks
as they often come with a poisonous attack.

9. cxd5

Mark wishes to give his queenside pieces some extra room and decides to exchange.

Lesson 12:

The exchange of pieces can be a good way to give your pieces more mobility.

In this instance, Mark prepares to put his rook on c1 and put long-term pressure on the c-file.

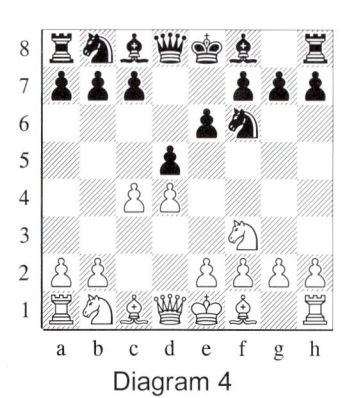

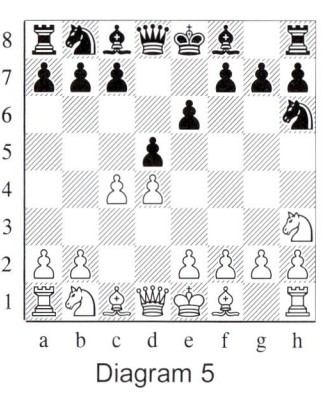

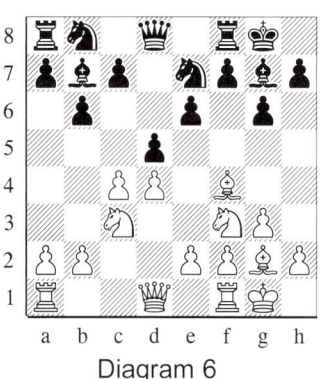

9. ...   Nxd5

10. Nxd5

10. ...   exd5

Roman recaptures with the central pawn blocking Mark's b7 bishop. You may well wonder why he does not capture with the bishop on b7. Taking with the bishop was also an option but Mark could respond with 11. Q-c2!, controlling the squares c7 & e4. Roman saw that he could not keep his bishop on d5 for long, as he could not stop e4. Here we see why it would have been better for Roman to develop his knight earlier, on the more natural f6 square.

11. R-c1

The exchange of pieces has given Mark a very nice half-open c-file which he immediately occupies with the rook.

Lesson 13:
Rooks work best on open files, but can also be powerful on half-open files.

11. ...   N-a6 (Diagram 7)

The black knight develops and defends the pawn on c7. But the knight is vulnerable here. Remember that the "knight on the rim is very dim"! If the knight had come to c6 (blocking the rook attack on the c7 pawn) the pinned knight and the blocked c7 pawn would become very weak and vulnerable to attack.

Lesson 14:
Rooks and queens work very well together.

12. b4!

At first glance it seems Mark is offering Roman the b4 pawn, but let's delve a little further!
The pawn on c7 is attacked twice by the rook on c7 and the bishop on f4. If Roman was to take this "poisoned pawn" Mark's rook could take on c7 attacking the bishop. Rooks on the 7th rank are best avoided as they can do an unmerciful amount of damage.

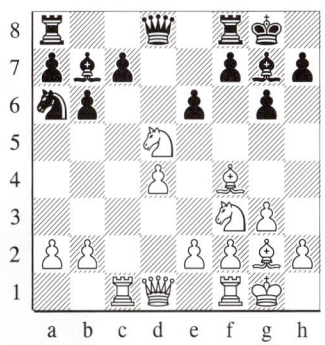

Diagram 7

12. ...   c6!

Roman wisely avoids taking the pawn and prevents Mark from getting his rook on the 7th rank. The resulting position for Roman is solid but slightly cramped. For the time being the knight on the rim does not have much space. If Roman gets the chance he will reroute his knight to e6 via c7 where his position will be ok. Mark must react quickly to prevent Roman from executing his plan.

13. Q-b3 (Diagram 8)

Mark protects the b4 pawn while exerting some extra pressure on the centre with his biggest cannon! Very nice Mark!

13. ...   R-e8

Very strategic! Roman's rook occupies the half-open e-file and threatens to take the pawn on e2. Is this enough to stop Mark from attacking in the centre?

14. Rf-e1!

Mark quietly defends his e2 pawn, keeping dreams of playing e4 and attacking Roman's centre alive.

14. ...   R-c8!

Why didn't Roman stick to his plan of playing N-c7 followed by N-e6? Ahhhh! There is a tactical problem! If 14. ... N-c7, Mark exchanges bishop for knight. After Qxc7, Mark would stun Roman with Qxd5!! with a big advantage for Mark (winning a pawn). Here you see the power of the rook on the half-open file. If cxd5, Rxc7. Roman's slow and awkward development gives Mark many attacking possibilities.

By playing R-c8, Roman prepares N-e6 via c7. Roman would of course love to free up his queenside position by pushing the c6 pawn to c5 but this would simply lose a pawn after bxc5. Roman cannot take back bxc5 because the white queen would capture the bishop on b7. By placing all of his pieces on natural squares Mark has created lots of opportunities for attack.

15. B-h3

Mark attacks the rook and provokes Roman to create a weakness.

15. ...   f5 (Diagram 9)

Roman blocks the attack. However in doing so, he has exposed the black king on the a2-g8 diagonal. It seems that Roman has come through the worst. The pawns on d5 & f5 control the key e4 square. Remember, whoever controls the centre controls the initiative! Roman may well have breathed a sigh of relief as it seems that he has survived the opening unscathed.

But Mark has a spectacular resource!

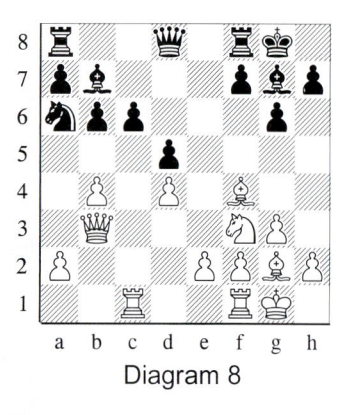

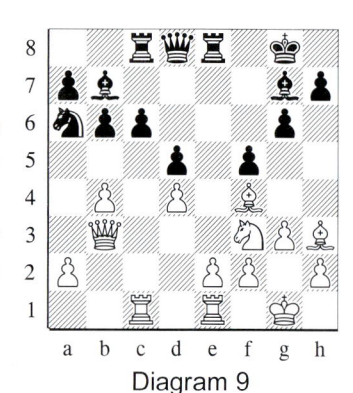

Here it is worth assessing the position from Mark's and from Roman's perspectives.

Mark needs to find a plan to take advantage of the following:
- Roman's queenside pieces (knight & bishop) are somewhat cramped.
- Mark's queen on b3 exerts x-ray pressure (through the pawn on d5) on the exposed black king on g8.
- Both of Roman's pawns on d5 and f5 are pinned.
- Roman's pawn on c6 is backward and potentially weak.

Roman can be happy with the following:
- His rook on e8 occupies the half-open e-file and seems to prevent the e4 break.
- His pawn structure seems solid and he is only two steps away from achieving his ideal position through N-c7-e6.

16. e4!! (Diagram 10)

This powerful move exploits the pins on the d5 and f5 pawns and smashes open the position. The d5 pawn cannot take on e4 because it is pinned against the king by the queen on b3. The f5 pawn cannot take on e4 as the white bishop would take the rook on c8. If 16. ... Rxe4, 17. Rxe4, fxe4; Roman still loses the rook for the bishop and pawn, or knight (f3) and pawn. If Roman ignores the pawn on e4 by K-h8, Mark simply plays exf5, gxf5, Bxf5 winning a pawn with a big attack.

16. ...   fxe4

Roman is in a very sticky position and decides that his best chance is to sacrifice his rook on c8 for Mark's powerful white squared bishop.

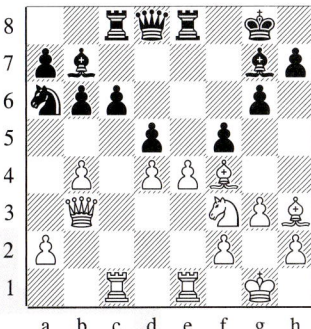

Diagram 10

17. N-g5!

Mark declines to take the rook on c8 and moves his knight to a powerful attacking position. The rook on c8 is still hanging and Mark can recapture the pawn on e4 at any time. Mark is now also threatening B-e6+ with a big attack. I like your style Mark!

Mark can of course immediately capture the c8 rook but Roman's resulting pawn on f3, after the capture of the knight (exf3), could be a dangerous pawn.

Many players starting out would immediately capture the rook and be grateful for the material advantage. Remember always that when you see a good move, be brave and try to find a better move. The first move that enters your head is usually the best but if you take your time there is often something more!

Lesson 15:
If you see a good move, take a moment to try and find a better one.

17. ...   N-c7

At last Roman finally get's his knight into the game and fights for the centre.

18. Rxe4!

Again, Mark thinks that he has found a plan that is better than capturing the rook. But how well has he worked it out? Sometimes in chess you have to give a little to get a lot but if you're not careful your opponent might escape. So what's going on in Mark's mind?

He sees:
- Mark's bishops are like rockets commanding the board.
- He sees his knight is perfectly placed to create havoc by jumping into e6.
- Roman's rook is attacked and his pieces are tied up in knots but is there a way to take advantage of this before Roman unravels?
- Roman's pawns are full of pins and threatened pins.

18. ...   Rxe4

19. Nxe4 (Diagram 11)

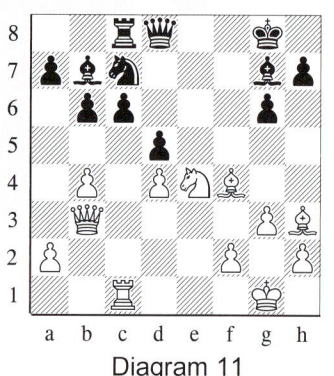

Diagram 11

The subject of piece mobility is a very important one in chess. It is not always true that the advantage lies with the player with the most piece mobility, but it is true most of the time. The more space a piece has, the more opportunity it has to attack and the more opportunity there is to restrict the opponent's forces. It is also easier to find combinations and bewilder your opponent with tactical flourishes. Now we'll look at the piece mobility in this game and the available moves on each side.

Pieces have their own specific values but look at how much more powerful Mark's bishops and knights are because of their mobility. We're not discussing the worth of pieces, only how much mobility they have and how they are working on the chessboard.

Diagram 12 notes the available moves for each piece. Mark has a lot more mobility and therefore makes it difficult for Roman to create a counter-attack.

How long will Roman be able to keep the position alive?

19. Piece Mobility

White		Black	
King	3	King	3
Queen	11	Queen	8
c1-Rook	9	c8-Rook	2
f4-Bishop	6	g7-Bishop	5
h3-Bishop	6	b7-Bishop	2
e4-Knight	6	c7-Knight	5
Total	**41**		**25**

Diagram 12

Lesson 16:
Watch piece mobility. Try to put your pieces on good attacking squares. Always try to improve the position of your pieces.

19. ...   R-b8

Roman is under pressure and cannot counter-attack so he decides to move his rook from danger and places it in a square where he can protect his bishop on b7.

Look at how the black bishop hasn't played any part in the game - this suggests that his idea to fianchetto both bishops may have been a mistake.

Lesson 17:
Bobby Fischer was a master at constantly making sure pieces were protected while manoeuvring them across the board. With this simple strategy, it should make looking after pieces a little simpler.

20. N-g5

The knight returns to the job of attacking the weak kingside.

20. ...   Bxd4

Roman can't think of anything better so he takes the pawn.
It is the final mistake!

21. Bxc7

It may seem strange that Mark should exchange his powerful black squared bishop for Roman's somewhat useless knight. Can Mark see something further down the line?

21. ...   Qxc7

Roman must recapture to keep the material even.

22. Qxd5+ (Diagram 13)

This is exactly what Mark was aiming for. Mark wins back a valuable pawn and sets up for the very powerful rook on the seventh rank. When there are less pieces on the board a rook on the seventh rank can be extremely dangerous. Doubled rooks on the seventh rank are almost irresistible in mating attacks. Now Mark thinks about playing for mate.

Lesson 18:
Rooks are very powerful on the seventh rank.

22. ...   cxd5

Roman is forced to exchange queens. If he moves his king Mark simply plays Qxd4 and is a piece up in a winning position. To avoid dropping a piece Roman must capture the queen and consequently allow Mark to get his rook on the seventh rank.

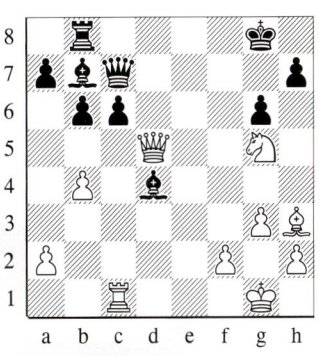

Diagram 13

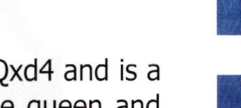

23. Rxc7

Mark recaptures with his rook and introduces the final weapon in his checkmating masterplan. The material is even but Mark's pieces have a lot more activity and attacking potential. Roman cannot move his rook as he would lose the bishop on b7 and Mark threatens to play Rxh7 or Nxh7.

Mark is not interested in pawns. He is going after the black king who has no pawns or pieces to defend him.

Lesson 19:
The idea of exchanging pieces when a pawn ahead is a good idea but one extra pawn may not always be enough to secure a winning position ("Stalemate", page 69).
When you are a pawn ahead, exchange pieces (queens, rooks, knights, bishops),
When you are a pawn down, exchange pawns!

23. ...   B-a6

The rook must be released from it's job protecting the white squared bishop. The rook surely has better things to do! Now Roman's a7 pawn is "en prise" and is sure to drop. This is Roman's' last attempt to get back into the game, but is it too late?

24. B-e6+

Whoops! Roman may have more to worry about than perhaps he first thought.

24. ...   K-f8 (Diagram 14)

The only move for Roman. The white rook is nicely placed so that the king cannot move from the first rank. The check cannot be blocked so Roman's options are slim! If 24. ... K-h8, 25. Rxh7#.
Even I'm feeling for poor Roman! See if you can find the final blow before continuing on.

25. R-f7+

Another nasty check! Roman's moves are now forced.

25. ...   K-e8

26. B-d7+

26. ...   Resigns (Diagram 15)

Roman's only move is K-d8 and checkmate immediately following with N-e6, Roman had no option but to throw in the towel!

1-0

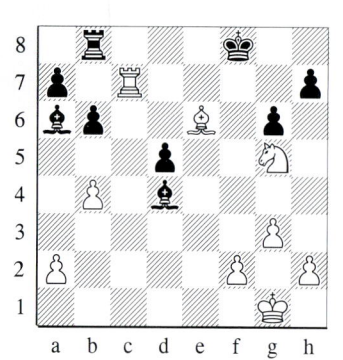

Diagram 14

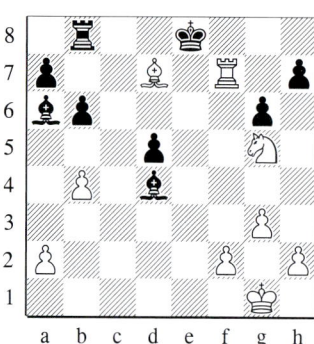

Diagram 15
The final position.
Can you see the checkmate that immediately follows?

Lessons from this Game

Now look at the lessons learned from this great game:

1: Make as few pawn moves as possible in the opening, focus on developing your pieces.
2: Don't move pawns without good reason.
3: If you play a move with a specific idea or plan be sure to follow through with your plan immediately before initiating a new plan or course of action.
4: In the opening try to have at least two ideas or reasons for every move.
5: Keep pressure on the centre.
6: Develop as early as possible by moving out your minor pieces early.
   Be careful with your queen - don't take her out too early as she might be chased, or worse still captured.
7: Place your pieces in a position where they have the most power and mobility. This is usually in the centre. - Sometimes however, a bishop on the long diagonal can be very powerful in a corner and exert pressure across the whole board.
8: Castle as quickly as possible.
9: In general it is best to develop knights before bishops but sometimes it depends on the opening plan of your opponent. Your bishops may be best placed in the centre as opposed to the long diagonal. Developing knights before bishops allows you configure best options for your bishops.
10: Place your pieces in a position where they have the most power and mobility, usually in the centre.
11: Watch all checks. Eliminate possible checks as they often come with a poisonous attack.
12: The exchange of pieces can be a good way to give your pieces more mobility.
13: Rooks work best on open files, but can also be powerful on half-open files.
14: Rooks and queens work very well together.
15: If you see a good move, take a moment to try and find a better one.
16: Watch piece mobility. Try to put your pieces on good attacking squares.
    Always try to improve the position of your pieces.
17: Bobby Fischer was a master at constantly making sure pieces were protected while manoeuvring them across the board. With this simple strategy, it should make looking after pieces a little simpler.
18: Rooks are very powerful on the seventh rank.
19: The idea of exchanging pieces when a pawn ahead is a good idea but one extra pawn may not always be enough to secure a winning position.
    - When you are a pawn ahead, exchange pieces (queens, rooks, knights, bishops),
    - When you are a pawn down, exchange pawns!

126

18 MORE PUZZLES

When you have mastered and become familiar with the ideas in this book try out the following puzzles.
Not for the faint-hearted!

Chess Puzzles 1
Simple

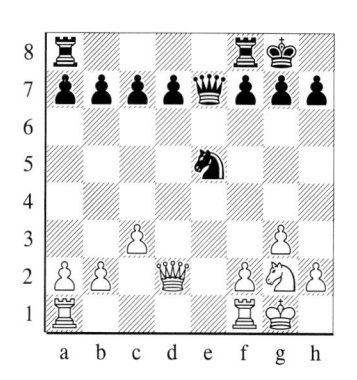

1

Fork:
How can Black capture the white queen?

Hint: A simple tactic may be deployed here.

Black's Move

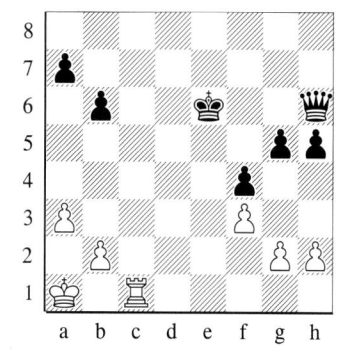

2

Skewer and a very dangerous check:
Black has a queen and White a rook. Is it possible for White to capture the black queen and win the game? How?

White's Move

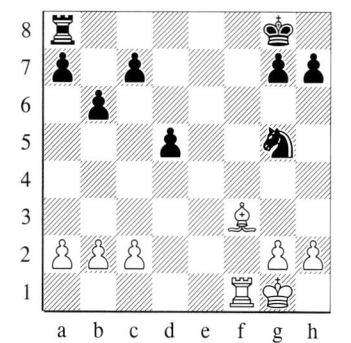

3

Fork:
How can White capture the black rook and win the game?

White's Move

Chess Puzzles 1
Simple

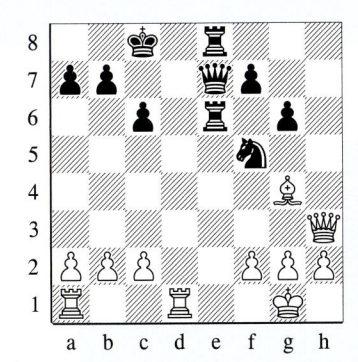

4

Back rank mate:
How can Black win the game?

Hint: Black has a lot of strength with the major pieces (queen and rooks) working together on the e-file.

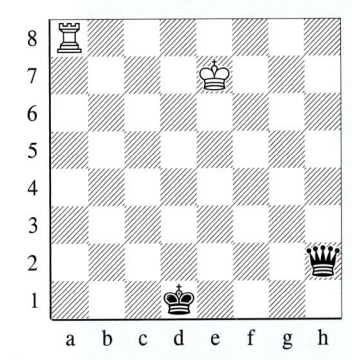

Black's Move

5

Skewer and a very dangerous check:
Black has a queen and White has the rook. How can White capture the black queen and win the game?

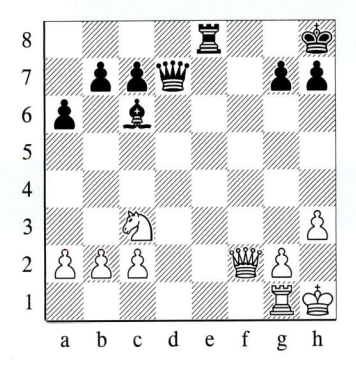

White's Move

6

Pin:
Find the very cunning checkmate for Black?

Black's Move

Chess Puzzles 2
Medium

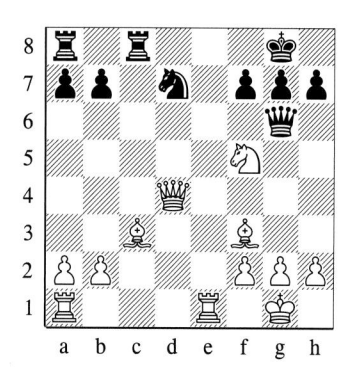

1 The black queen is attacking the white knight. Is White in danger or do you see how White can do something very clever?

Hint: Maybe there's a clever move from the white knight, a fork perhaps. Then try and find the checkmate.

White's Move ○

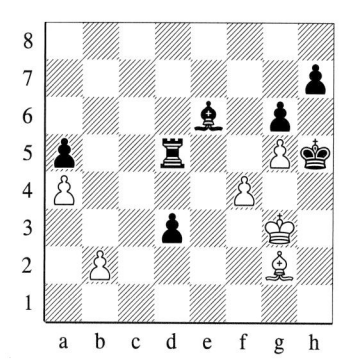

2

The black pawn is moving towards the final rank but White has another plan. Does White have an opportunity for checkmate?

White's Move ○

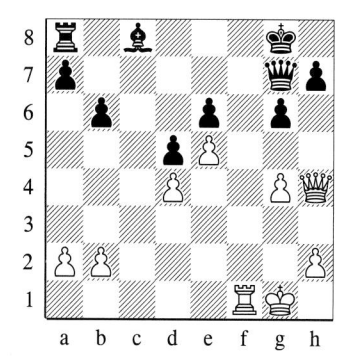

3

Black has an extra bishop in this position but the rook is restricted. Do you see how White can win?

Hint: The white queen has lots of space! And the rook has lots of power on the open file.

White's Move ○

Chess Puzzles 2
Medium

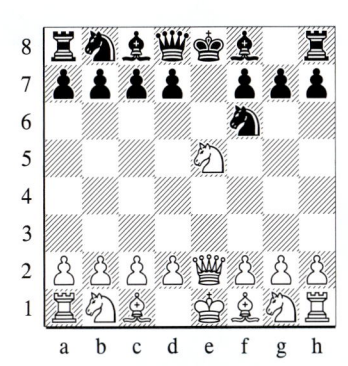

4

Discovered check:
The game has just begun but already Black is in trouble.
1. e4, e5; 2. N-f3, N-f6; 3. Nxe5, Nxe4; 4. Q-e2, N-f6.
Can you see how White can capture Black's queen?

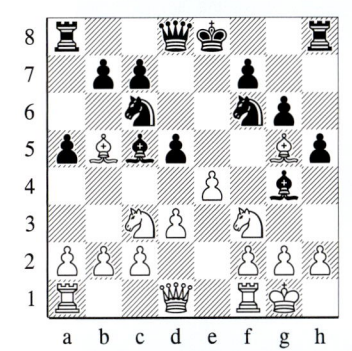

White's Move

5

Pin
The black knight on c6 and the black knight on f6 are pinned. Can White exploit this advantage and win a piece?
Hint: There are two answers to this puzzle!

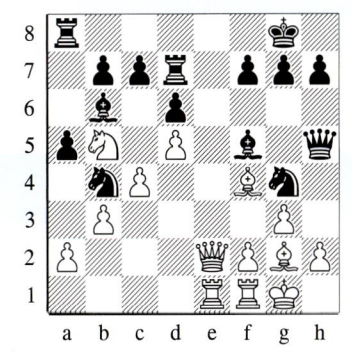

White's Move

6

Power of the rook and queen working together:
Black would like to checkmate on h2 but White has another plan. Can White inflict checkmate first?

White's Move

Chess Puzzles 3
Hard

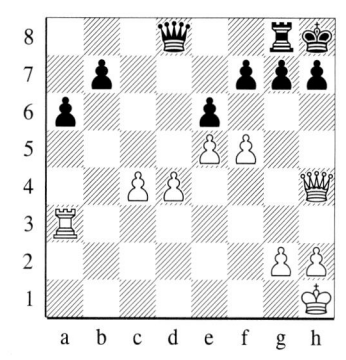

1

White to play and mate in three.

White's Move

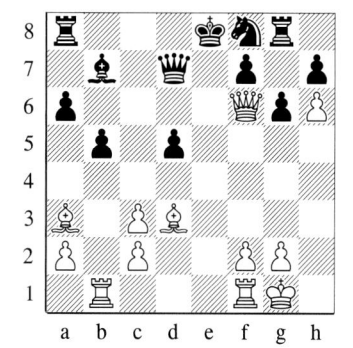

2

Black is in quite a bit of danger here. Black has not yet castled and White is attacking the black squares. Can White win a piece with this attack?

YES!!! But how?

White's Move

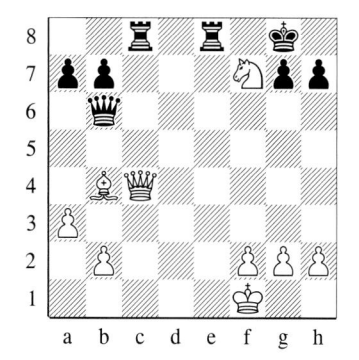

3

White can force a draw with
1. N-h6+, K-h8;
2. N-f7+, K-g8;
3. N-h6+, K-h8... perpetual check!
Does White have a better option?

YES!!! But what?

White's Move

Chess Puzzles 3
Hard

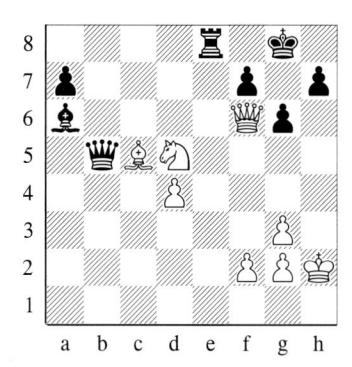

4 Black is weak on the black squares. How can White exploit this weakness for his / her own benefit?

Hint: The g7 square is very weak for Black. Can White exploit this weakness?

White's Move ○

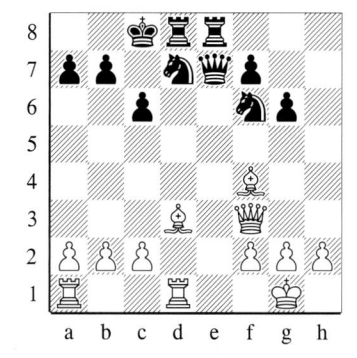

5 Is Black comfortable here? You would think so but there is a definite weakness. White's bishops are very strong and Black's king is restricted. Do you see how White can win?

Hint: The black king does not have a legal move in this position. Can White exploit this weakness?

White's Move ○

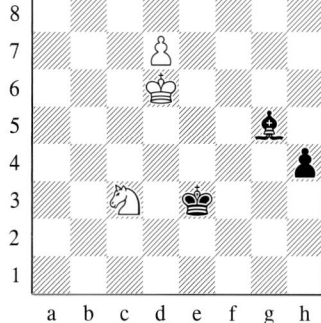

6 Both White and Black are trying to promote pawns.
How can White safely get a queen before Black promotes?

White's Move ○

134

19
PUZZLES & LESSONS
- ANSWERS

Lesson 1

Page 18

Check

1 Bishop on h5	**2** Knight on c7	**3** Rook on d1
4 Queen on a4	**5** Pawn on e4	**6** Knight on e7

Lesson 2

Page 21

Moving the Pieces 1

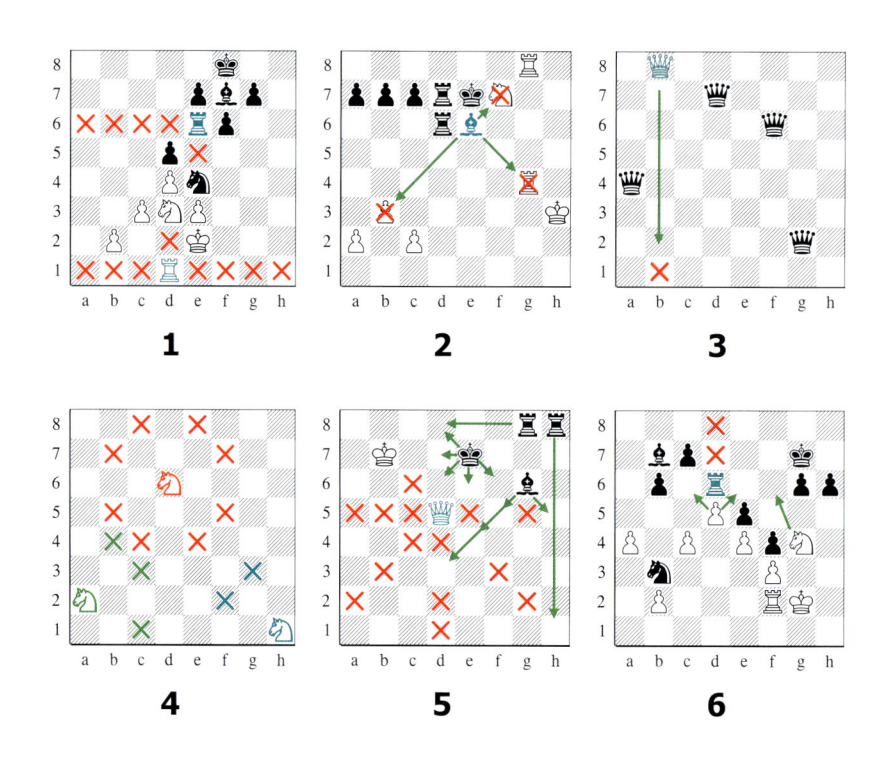

Lesson 6

Page 25

Moving the Pieces 2

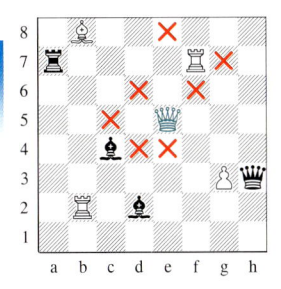

1

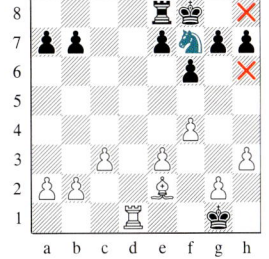

2

5. dxe is not permitted in puzzle 5 as White would be moving into check (from the b7 bishop), which is illegal.
6. In puzzle 6 Black's bishop cannot move as Black would be exposing a check from the white rook on e1. It is illegal in chess to move into check.

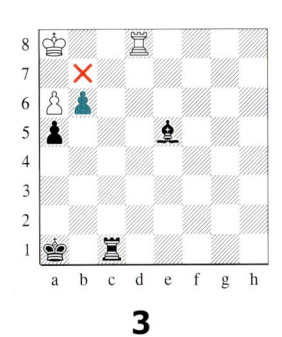

3

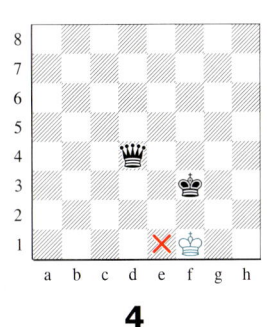

4

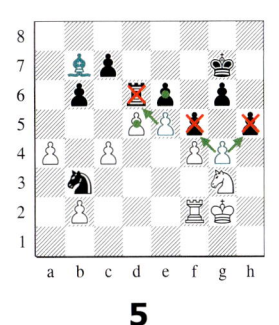

5

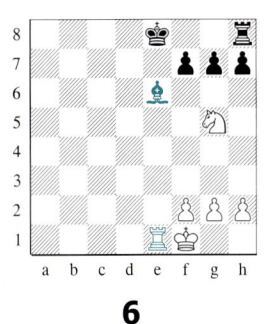

6

Lesson 7

Page 26

Moving the Pieces 3

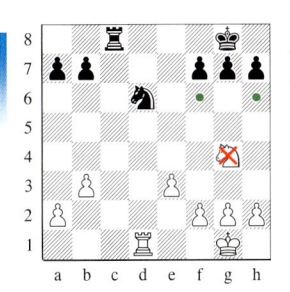

1

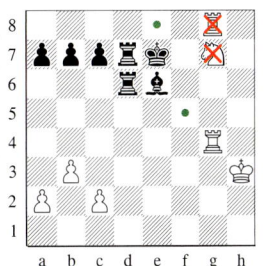

2

• In puzzle 6 the bishop on c2 cannot move at all as Black would be moving into check (from the c8 rook) which is illegal. Therefore the only white piece that can put the king in check is the rook on d1.

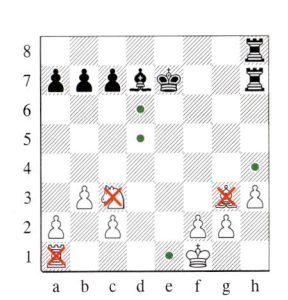

3

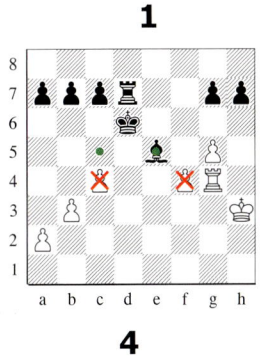

4

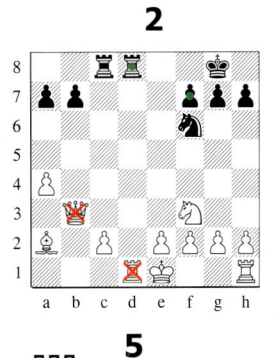

5

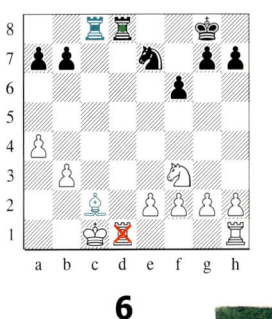

6

Lesson 8

Page 31

Value of the Pieces

4 ♟ + ♟
5 ♟ + ♟ + ♟
6 ♜ + ♙ or ♘ + ♘ or ♗ + ♗ or ♘ + ♗
7 ♜
8 ♜ + ♙ or ♘ + ♘ or ♗ + ♗ or ♘ + ♗
9 ♙,   10 ♙
11 ♜,   12 ♕

13 ♘ or ♗
14 ♙ + ♙
15 ♜ + ♜
16 ♜, ♗ or ♘
17 ♕ + ♙
18 ♙ + ♙ + ♙
19 ♕

Lesson 9

Page 47

Checkmate Puzzles

1. Qxh7#
2. Q-g8#
3. Nxc7#
4. N-f7#
5. ...Qxh2#
6. ...R-d8# or o-o-o#
7. Q-d7#
8. N-e7#
9. ...R-e1#
10. ...f2#
11. Q-b7#
12. Bxh3#
13. N-e4+, K-d7; Q-c8#
14. ...Q-b1+; Q-g1, Qxg1#
15. R-g8+, N-g6; Bxg6#
16. Rxh2+, K-f1; R-d1# or R-h1#
17. R-d7+, K-f8 or K-g8; Q-g7#
18. K-b6, K-b8; R-h8#
19. B-b2+, Qxb2; Qxb2#
20. e8=N+, K-h8; Bxf6#

Lesson 10

Page 87

The Pawn

ISOLATED PAWN?
White: e3 / Black: d6

DOUBLED PAWNS?
White: none / Black: f6 & f7

TRIPLE PAWNS?
White: c2, c3, c4 / Black: none

Backward Pawn?
White: c2, c3 / Black: f7

Passed Pawn?
White: none / Black: a5

Lesson 11

Page 89

Tactics

Tactical Move	Tactic Name	Piece Won	Points Won
1. ♘xf7	1. Fork	1. Queen + Pawn	9+1=10
2. ♖-b8+	2. Skewer	2. Queen	9
3. ♗-d4+	3. Skewer	3. Rook	5
4. ♗xd6+	4. Fork	4. Rook+ Pawn for a Bishop	5+1-3=3
5. ♘-c6+	5. Discovered check	5. Queen for a Knight	9-3=6
6. d5	6. Fork	6. Rook for a Pawn	5-1=4
7. ♘-e7+	7. Fork	7. Rook for a Knight	5-3=2
8. d5	8. Pin	8. Knight	3

Lesson 13

Page 97

The Passed Pawn in the Endgame

White first	Black first
1. g6, hxg6	1. g6, fxg6
2. f6, gxf6	2. h6, gxh6
3. h6, passed pawn.	3. f6, passed pawn.

Answers to Chess Puzzles

Simple - 1
(page 128)

1. <u>1</u>. ..., N-f3+; <u>2</u>. K-h1, Nxd2.
2. <u>1</u>. R-c6+; K-(rank 5 or 7), 2. Rxh6.
3. <u>1</u>. Bxd5+, K-h8 or f8; <u>2</u>. Bxa8: Black cannot save the rook. As a result it is easy for White to eat up the remaining black pawns with the extra rook and promote a white pawn to win the game.
4. <u>1</u>. ..., R-e1+; <u>2</u>. Rxe1, Qxe1+; <u>3</u>. Rxe1, Rxe1#.
5. <u>1</u>. R-a1+, K-(rank 2); <u>2</u>. R-a2+, K-(rank 1 or 3); <u>3</u>. Rxh2.
6. <u>1</u>. ..., Qxh3#. The g2 pawn is pinned.

Medium - 2
(page 130)

1. <u>1</u>. N-e7+, K-f8 or h8; <u>2</u>. Nxg6+, K-g8 or f-pawn or h-pawn captures the knight on g6; <u>3</u>. Qxg7#.
2. <u>1</u>. B-f3+, B-g4; Bxg4#.
3. <u>1</u>. Q-d8+, Q-f8; <u>2</u>.Qxf8#.
4. <u>1</u>. ..., N-c6+(discovered check from White's queen on e2); Black can move Q-e7 but the queen is still lost.
5. <u>1</u>. exd5 or e5, the knights cannot move as they are pinned.
6. <u>1</u>. ..., Q-e8+, Rxe8, <u>2</u>.Rxe8#.

Hard - 3
(page 132)

1. <u>1</u>. Qxh7+, Kxh7; <u>2</u>. R-h3+, Q-h4; Rxh4#.
2. <u>1</u>. Q-g7!! If Rxg7, the pawn on h6 can capture the rook and promote quite easily. If Black does not take the queen, the rook is lost.
3. <u>1</u>. N-h6+, K-h8; <u>2</u>. Q-g8+, Rxg8; <u>3</u>. N-f7#.
4. <u>1</u>. B-f8 (planning Q-g7#); if Rxf8, <u>2</u>. N-e7#; if Kxf8, <u>2</u>. Q-h8#.
5. <u>1</u>. Qxc6+, bxc6; <u>2</u>. B-a6#.
6. <u>1</u>. N-d5+, K– anywhere; <u>2</u>. N-e7 and blocking Black's control on d8.

20 CHESS PUZZLE FROM NEW ZEALAND!

This chess puzzle is really fascinating - try it!
Don't worry, the answer is here as well!!

Chess Puzzle from New Zealand!

The answer's in the tractor!

My brother Donal O Boyle, a keen chess player, lived in New Zealand some years ago and came across the following story in a New Zealand newspaper in 1990:

This story comes from Israel Parry, a recent visitor to New Zealand from San Francisco.

In a remote Russian village about 30 years ago, two masters were playing in a local club. White considered it a lost position and so resigned. A local farmer, who witnessed this, was intrigued by the final position, so he made a note of it and later studied it at home.

Not immediately finding anything exciting, he placed the position in his tractor. There it accompanied him on his ploughing chores for many years, the farmer glancing at it intermittently.

After approximately 20 years, the farmer discovered an incredible resource that in fact gave White a forced win. He wrote a letter to the club explaining his remarkable find. A club official received the letter, read it, and filed it away.

In December 1986, former world champion Mikhail Tal happened to be in this village, and looking through the club archives came across the letter. He confirmed the correctness of the analysis and was so impressed that he wrote a letter to the farmer's family in the hope of arranging a meeting with him.

Tal found out in reply that the farmer had died some years previously.

The diagram shows the final game position.

White to play and win.

The solution is a little difficult to find, but well worth the effort, since it is one of the most magnificent, beautiful and profound combinations in the history of chess.

The answer is on the following page...

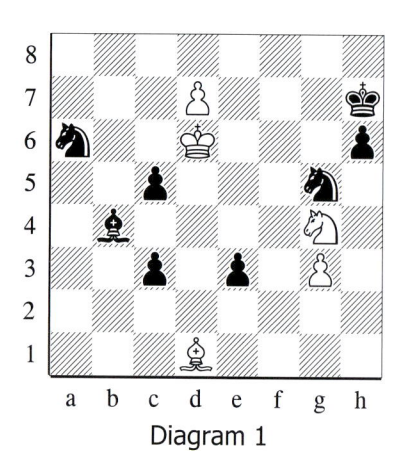

Diagram 1

Answer to the chess problem from New Zealand

The answer's in the tractor!

The answer:
1. **N-f6+, K-g7**; (if 1. ...K-g6 2. B-h5+ and the d7 pawn safely promotes, 3. d8=Q),
    - note the threat of N-f7 forking the king and promoted pawn on d8.
2. **N-h5+, K-g6**; (if 2. ...K-h7 3. B-c2+,
    if 3. ...K-h8, 4. B-b3 and the d7 pawn safely promotes.
    Or if 3. ...K-g8, 4. B-b3+ and the d7 pawn safely promotes).
3. **B-c2+!!**, (The key move in the first phase of the combination).
3. ..., **Kxh5**; (if 3. ...K-f 7 4. d8=Q)
4. **d8=Q! N-f7+**; (Otherwise white retains a decisive material advantage).
5. **K-e6, Nxd8+**;
6. **K-f5**, (The first phase is finished). White is now threatening 7. B-d1#.
    6. ..., **e2; blocking B-d1# and Black now threatens to promote.**
7. **B-e4!**, (The beginning of the bishop's second mighty journey). White again threatens B-f3 checkmate.
    7. ..., **e1=N**; (the only way to stop checkmate).
8. **B-d5!!**, White is three pieces down and the king out in the open. White still has enough time to attack with B-c4 then B-e2 checkmate. Black's next two moves stop this checkmate. Strangely, he cannot check the white king to escape this attack despite the considerable material advantage.

8. ..., **c2, again threatening to promote;**
9. **B-c4, c1=N** (again the only way to stop checkmate).
10. **B-b5!, N-c7**; (to stop 11. B-e8#)
11. **B-a4**, with 12. B-d1 checkmate following.
    Black is cornered! The white bishop is running rings around the four knights!

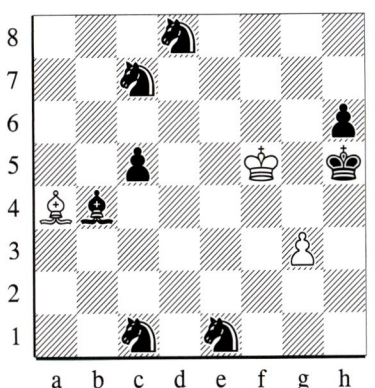

Diagram 2

Here is the unbelievable journey of the white bishop:

d1-c2-e4-d5-c4-b5-a4-d1#

144

Section 5

Chess Terms   **147**
Chess in Different Languages   **151**
Reference Material   **153**

146

21
CHESS TERMS

It's time to learn the official terms in chess.

Chess Terms

Capture	When a piece is captured and removed from the game.
Counter Attack	An attack which is implemented when an enemy attack is underway.
Check	When the king is under attack from an enemy piece.
Checkmate	If the king cannot escape from check.
Defend	The protection of a piece in the face of an attack or a potential attack.
Development	Taking pieces out where they are more mobile and more powerful.
Discovered check	A position where a piece moves to expose a check from another piece.
Discovered attack	A position where a piece moves to expose an attack from another piece.
Double attack	Two pieces under attack from the same enemy piece.
Double check	A position where the king is in check from two different pieces.
En Passant	A special pawn move where an enemy pawn is captured (page 62).
En Prise	Pronounced *en-pree*. A piece is "en prise" when it is under attack by an enemy piece and is unprotected.
Exchange	Where both sides capture pieces.
Fianchetto	A pattern where the developed bishop is on the second rank on the knight's file.
File	The squares up and down the chess board.
Forced Move	The only possible move.
Fork	A type of double attack.
Gambit	An opening in which a piece (usually a pawn) is offered as a sacrifice, to get an advantage later in the game.
Illegal Move	A move that is not allowed; one that breaks the rules of chess.
J'adoube	Said by chess players when they wish to let their opponent know that they are settling a piece correctly in its square and don't wish to move it.
Minor Piece	Bishop or knight.
Major Piece	Queen or rook.
Open File	A file without pawns.
Opening	The opening moves.
Passed Pawn	A pawn that is free from enemy pawns directly or diagonally in front of it. The objective of a passed pawn is to promote (page 93).
Pawn Promotion	When a pawn reaches the end of the board and changes to another piece (page 60).
Protected Passed Pawn	A passed pawn that is protected by another pawn.
Pin	A piece is pinned when it cannot move without exposing another piece (usually of higher value) to attack.

Fianchetto

...Chess Terms

Rank The squares across the chess board.

Stalemate A position in which the player to move cannot make a legal move. The only options are illegal moves; this is a drawn game.

Zwischenzug A Zwischenzug is a common chess tactic where a player, instead of playing the expected move (commonly a recapture of a piece), first makes another move posing an immediate threat that the opponent must answer. The expected move is then played.
This in-between move is called a Zwischenzug.

Zwischenschach A Zwischenschach is a chess tactic where a player, instead of playing the expected move, first makes a check that the opponent must answer. The expected move follows.
This in-between check is called a Zwischenschach.

Zugzwang A player must move even though it will make his/her position worse; it would be much better to pass on the move, although we know that is not allowed in chess.

Chess Titles

Title	
GM	Grandmaster
WGM	Woman Grandmaster
IM	International Master
WIM	Woman International Master
FM	FIDE Master
WFM	Woman FIDE Master
NM	National Master
CM	Candidate Master
WCM	Woman Candidate Master

FIDE
FIDE is the governing body for world chess.
FIDE: Fédération Internationale des Echecs - French for "World Chess Federation".

150

22
CHESS IN DIFFERENT LANGUAGES

Now! Would you like to learn the names of the pieces in different languages?

Chess in Different Languages

English	chess	pawn	knight	bishop	rook	queen	king
Bulgarian	sah	peska	kon	ofitser	top	dama	tsar
Catalan	escacs	peó	cavall	alfil	torre	dama	rei
Croatian	šah	pješak	skakač	lovac	top	dama	kralj
Czech	šachy	pěšec	jezdec	střelec	věž	dáma	král
Danish	skak	bonde	springer	løber	tårn	dronning	konge
Dutch	schaken	pion	paard	loper	toren	dame	koning
Estonian	male	soldur	ratsu	oda	vanker	lipp	kuningas
Finnish	šakki / shakki	sotilas	ratsu	lähetti	torni	kuningatar	kuningas
French	échecs	pion	cavalier	fou	tour	dame	roi
German	Schach	Bauer	Springer	Läufer	Turm	Dame	König
Greek	skaki	pioni	ippos	axiomatikos	pyrgos	vasilissa	vasilias
Hungarian	sakk	gyalog	huszár	futó	bástya	vezér	király
Icelandic	skák	peð	riddari	biskup	hrókur	drottning	kóngur
Irish	ficheall	ceitearnach	ridire	easpag	caiseal	banríon	rí
Italian	scacchi	pedone	cavallo	alfiere	torre	donna	re
Latin	ludus latruncularius	pedes	eques	cursor	turris	regina	rex
Latvian	sahs	bandinieks	zirdzis	laidnis	torris	dama	karalis
Lithuanian	šachmatai	pėstininkas	žirgas	rikis	bokštas	valdovė	karalius
Luxembourgish	Schach	Bauer	Päerd	Leefer	Tuerm	Damm	Kinnek
Māori	whaikīngi	kaihāpai-ō	toa	pīhopa	pā tūwatawata	kuīni	kīngi
Norwegian	sjakk	bonde	springer	løper	tårn	dronning	konge
Persian	chatrang	piyada	asp	pil	rukh	farzin	shah
Polish	szachy	pionek	skoczek	goniec	wieża	hetman	król
Portuguese	xadrez	peão	cavalo	bispo	torre	rainha	rei
Romanian	şah	pion	cal	nebun	turn	dama / regina	rege
Russian	schamaty	peshka	kon	slon	ladja	ferz	korol
Scots Gaelic	taileasg	ceatharnach	ridir	easbuig	caisteal	banrighinn	righ
Slovak	sach	pesiak	kol	strelec	veda	dama	sach
Slovene	sah	kmet	konji	teka	stolp	dama	kral
Spanish	ajedrez	peón	caballo	alfil	torre	reina	rey
Swedish	schack	bonde	springare	löpare	torn	drottning	kung
Thai	makruk	bia	ma	khon	rua	met	khun
Turkish	satranç	piyon	at	fil	kale	vezir	sah
Ukrainian	sahy	pisak	kin	slon	tura	koroleva	korol
Welsh Gaelic	gwyddbwyll	gwerinwr	marchog	esgob	castell	brenhines	teyrn / brenin

23
REFERENCE MATERIAL

Here are a few ideas on how to improve your chess even more.

REFERENCES

This chess book is an adopted translation of the first ever chess book in the Irish language,
    FICHEALL - Úna O Boyle (published in 2010 by Úna O Boyle)
    FICHEALL was shortlisted for Irish language children's book of the year, Gradam Réics Carló 2011.
Logical Chess: move by move - Irving Chernev (Batsford 1998)
New Zealand Press; Evening Post - 1990
ESB Checkmate - Michael Crowe
Chess Lessons - Elizabeth Shaughnessy (The Berkeley Chess School - www.berkeleychessschool.org)
Chess players around the world who helped with "Chess in Different Languages".

RECOMMENDATIONS

BOOKS:

How to Play Chess like an Animal - *Brian Wall and Anthea Caerson;* (Mother's House Publishing, 2007).
ISBN-10: 0979714478; **ISBN**-13: 978-0979714474**.**

Chess For Tigers - *Simon Webb;* (Oxford University Press, 1978).
ISBN-10: 0080377882; **ISBN**-13: 978-0080377889**.**

Logical Chess: move by move - *Irving Chernev;* (Batsford, 1998).
ISBN-10: 0671211358; **ISBN**-13: 978-0671211356**.** (medium advanced)

Understanding the Chess Openings - *Sam Collins;* (Gambit Publications, 2005).
ISBN-10: 190460028X; **ISBN**-13: 978-1904600282**.** (advanced)

How to Reassess your Chess (4th edition) - *Jeremy Silman;* (Siles Press, 2010).
ISBN-10: 1890085138; **ISBN**-13: 978-1890085131**.** (advanced)

The March of Chess Ideas - *Anthony Saidy;* (e+Chess, 2013).
This is an interactive ebook available on epluschess.com which can be explored on your digital tablet.
Originally published by Random House Puzzles and Games in 1994. **ISBN**-13: 978-1927179093**.** (advanced)

INTERNET SITES

FIDE, Chess in Schools - www.cis.fide.com
Moves For Life (Ireland) - www.movesforlife.ie
Chess in Schools and Communities - www.chessinschools.co.uk
4 Nations Chess League - www.4ncl.co.uk
www.glorneycupchess.org
www.chesskid.com
www.chesskids.org.uk
www.chess.com
www.chessdrum.net
www.chessgames.com
www.gingergm.com

Be sure you have a parent or guardian with you when conversing or playing online.

ONLINE CHESS SUPPLIES

www.chess.co.uk
www.wholesalechess.co.uk
www.regencychess.co.uk
www.chesszsales.net
www.chesseire.com

PLAYING CHESS ONLINE

The best way to improve your chess is to play and play again and again. You can play chess on the internet with people from around the world throughout the day, round the clock. People of all ages and skills play online.

CHESS FEDERATIONS AND WEBSITES

FIDE - Fédération Internationale des Echecs - World Chess Federation - www.fide.com
ECU - European Chess Union - www.europechess.net
ECF - English Chess Federation - www.englishchess.org.uk
ICU - Irish Chess Union - www.icu.ie
ICO - Irish Chess Organisation - www.irishchess.org
UCU - Ulster Chess Union - www.ulsterchess.org
WCU - Welsh Chess Union - www.welshchessunion.com
CS - Chess Scotland - www.chessscotland.com
Jersey Chess - www.jerseychessclub.com
Guernsey Chess - www.guernseychessclub.org.gg
Isle of Man Chess - www.iomchess.com
USCF - The United States Chess Federation - www.uschess.org
For more information visit www.worldchesslinks.net

The Author
WCM Úna O Boyle

Úna was born and raised in the village of Duleek, County Meath, Ireland. Her father, Enda, taught chess to her and her siblings when they were young. Chess became an integral part of family life for Úna, with two older brothers who were only too happy to exploit her tactical weaknesses as a beginner.

As a young adult Úna worked as a product designer in New York, London and Dublin, where she now lives. Chess took a back seat for some years and in the 1990s music was to become her main creative outlet releasing several albums to critical acclaim (unaoboyle.net).

Úna returned to chess a few years later and began participating in competitions throughout the country. She represented Ireland at the Chess Olympiads in Dresden in 2008 (where she won the Women's Candidate Master title) and Khanty Mansiysk in 2010. At the same time she also started teaching in Irish language schools. It was in these classes that she got the inspiration for the Irish language version of this book, FICHEALL. Úna has brought an innovative style to teaching and promoting chess, and to date has run numerous highly successful national events for young players in various schools and notably in Dublin's Mansion House.

(photograph: Gianni Mersch)

For many years Úna has been at the core of chess in Ireland through her work on the executive of the Irish Chess Union. She was central in bringing the legendary grandmaster Garry Kasparov to Ireland in 2014, which led to a fresh upsurge of Irish media interest in chess.

Úna has also tutored in the prison system in Ireland where chess is now flourishing. She continues to work in Irish Chess and in schools motivating further generations to play and be enthralled by this wonderful game.

Úna, competing at the Dresden Olympiad.
(photographs: Chris Tandy and Dr. Daaim Shabazz, www.chessdrum.net)